In This Place

In This Place

Reflections on the Land of the Gospels
for the Liturgical Cycles

Marianne Race, C.S.J.
Laurie Brink, O.P.

WIPF & STOCK · Eugene, Oregon

Wipf and Stock Publishers
199 W 8th Ave, Suite 3
Eugene, OR 97401

In This Place
Reflections on the Land of the Gospels for the Liturgical Cycles
By Race, Marianne, CSJ, and Brink, Laurie, OP
Copyright©1998 by Race, Marianne, CSJ, and Brink, Laurie, OP
ISBN 13: 978-1-55635-906-4
Publication date 3/19/2008
Previously published by The Liturgical Press, 1998

DEDICATION

To Joan and Brad Brink, Sr.,
whose holy and adventuresome spirits have encouraged my own.
—L.B.

In memory of Mary Heffernan Race and Cyril Race, Sr.,
who nurtured me in the faith.
—M.R.

Contents

Reflections on the Sunday Cycles

Foreword

This book is a work of love by two women who have come to know and love the Land of the Bible as their own. They have traversed its hills and valleys and guided many others along its sacred ways. They have studied its archaeological treasures, prayed at its many holy sites, experienced its ever-present contradictions, and established lasting bonds of friendship with the people of this Land. In short, they have stood "in this place"—and they have come to love it.

The descriptions and reflections that they share in these pages invite every reader into the Land, to stand "in this place" with them. But like Moses before the burning bush, one must first remove sandals and acknowledge that the ground is holy. "What makes this so?" the authors ask. Their answer is rich and satisfying. "Every sacred place is a place where transcendence is possible," where one encounters the divine. If this is potentially true of every space, how much more is it the case with the biblical land of Israel/Palestine? After a short reflection on sacred space and the holiness of the Land, Part One concludes with a brief and helpful summary of the biblical tradition and its ongoing saga in the Land.

In Part Two, the Gospel stories, so familiar and yet so strange, come alive in new ways against the contours of the Land. For each of the thirty-six places mentioned in the Gospel texts of the three liturgical cycles, there is a picture and a detailed, physical description of the *place,* followed by a reflection on the Gospel scenes that are set in that place. And so we come to feel with John the Baptist the scorching sun of the Judean Wilderness, its parched earth and desolate surroundings. With Mary we learn to walk the terraced hillsides of Ein Karem in search of Elizabeth, and we see with the eyes of Jesus the entire outline of the city of Jerusalem spread out across the horizon from the Mount of Olives. The details of the topography, climate, and setting enrich our hearing of these Gospel stories in wonderful ways.

As we all know, *places* seep into our souls. And for Marianne Race and Laurie Brink, the Holy Land has done just that. It is from this *interior place* that they share their own personal reflections on the meaning of the Gospel texts enlightened by their knowledge of the Land. The narrow, winding streets of the Old City of Jerusalem, the ubiquitous basalt boulders of Upper Galilee, and the abundant springs of En Gedi have all become familiar friends to them. Since 1991 Marianne has been the Program Director of the Israel Study Programs at Catholic Theological Union in Chicago, having been a participant herself in the 1988 Fall Program. Every fall for the past eight years she has accompanied groups for eleven weeks in the Holy Land and has helped them to know this biblical landscape. Laurie participated in the 1994 Fall Program and since that time has three times returned to Israel as a member of the Combined Caesarea Expeditions archaeological team, which is "unearthing the past" in Herod's great harbor city of Caesarea. Over the next five years she will return each summer to register material culture for this project. Readers will surely find, in Marianne and Laurie, two trusted guides to the biblical land of Israel/Palestine and to the word of the Gospel that began there.

It is a great privilege and joy for me to recommend *In This Place*. This book is a welcome aid to our imaginations as we try to "picture Jesus" by the sea or on the mountainside or in the house of Peter. It is nourishment for our prayer, because the familiar texts become suddenly new, and we hear from the heart of these Gospels the voice of Jesus calling to us again. Most of all, this book delights us because we discover that in walking the Land with Jesus, we, too, have (as T. S. Eliot would say) "arrived at where we started," knowing that we are *In this Place* "for the first time."

BARBARA E. BOWE, R.S.C.J.

Introduction

Pilgrimage and Place

The advent of invisible highways of communication and instant connections across oceans have shortened the distance from here to anywhere. Whether we are in search of conversation or information, technology can now provide ready access. Though we can reach out and touch each other, often our attempts to touch the divine fall short. The saying "You had to be there" serves as an apt metaphor for spiritual life at the crossroads of this new millennium. We desire desperately to "be there," but we are often lost on the way. Whether rediscovering ancient spiritual practices like the Labyrinth or walking the paths of New Age religion, we yearn for the transcendent, the holy.

But we do not want some ethereal encounter—we hunger for the tangible. The way the bread and wine can be ritual and reality, so too can place. For Christians, the place has often been divorced from our spirituality. We live in a new realm, not bound by the Torah or situated by location but transformed in Christ as "creation awaits with eager expectation the revelation of the children of God" (Rom 8:19). The Jesus of history and place has far too long been subsumed into the Christ of faith.

Early in Christianity's formative years, encountering the physical world of Jesus and the Apostles became important. After the conversion of Constantine, pilgrims began traversing the Mediterranean world to "return" to the Holy Land of Palestine. The anonymous journal of the Bordeaux Pilgrim records a journey in 333.[1] The Pilgrimage of Egeria, probably written between 381 and 384, recounts a woman's travels to the Holy Land.[2] Archaeology attests to the renovation of a common house in Capernaum as early as the mid-first century. Suc-

---

[1] The Bordeaux Pilgrim (333) made a journey from Bordeaux to Jerusalem and back by way of Rome to Milan. His is the oldest pilgrim account and is called Itinerarium a Burdigala Hierusalem usque (Jack Finegan, The Archaeology of the New Testament (Princeton, N.J.: Princeton University Press, 1992) xvii.

[2] Jonathan Z. Smith, To Take Place (Chicago: University of Chicago Press, 1987) 89.

cessive constructions resulted in what is easily identifiable as a church built over what early believers held to be the home of St. Peter.

With literature and archaeology abundant, we can see that the places made "holy" by the birth of Christianity and the presence of Judaism were important to the early followers of Jesus. Making a pilgrimage became a significant response to one's belief. Alphonse Dupront called pilgrimage the "therapy of distance."[3] The spiritual needs of the individual could not be met locally, and thus the experience of travel, often dangerous travel, allowed a sufficient travail, an asceticism of sorts, engendering in the pilgrim a sense of both personal atonement and personal enlightenment. "The arduous task of journey to Palestine and its holy sites," writes David Satran, fulfilled this "therapy of distance." But for those who could not embark on such journeys, literature about the Holy Land "provides exactly that sense of proximity by bringing the prophets and their physical setting directly to the reader of the text." Satran suggests this makes "the geography of Scripture tangible from afar."[4]

The land in which our Christian story first took root remains fertile soil for our spirituality. As Satran says, literature can make the "geography of Scripture tangible from afar." The hope of this book is twofold: to make the land tangible for those who have been there and those who may never go, and to situate the Sunday gospels in a specific locality so as to "ground" the story more solidly. When Egeria first set out on her pilgrimage, she did so with a plan. "There is an incipient liturgical pattern to Egeria's experience of a place: she arrives at a place noteworthy in scripture; a prayer is said; this is followed by a reading of the biblical passage 'proper' to the place (given her itinerary, usually from the Hebrew Bible, and usually from the Pentateuch); then a psalm appropriate to the place is recited; and the proceedings conclude with a final prayer."[5]

So, too, with this book, there is a pattern. Each entry provides the reader with recent archaeological information so as to ground the gospel. Then, in light of the passages from the Sunday Scripture, what is "holy" about that site today will be discussed. For those who have walked the dusty roads of Palestine, this may serve to stimulate your own memories. For those for whom Jerusalem is merely a name, this will give you a "feel" for the land called "Holy." The greatest concern

[3]Peter Brown, *The Cult of the Saints* (Chicago: University of Chicago Press, 1981) 86–87.

[4]David Satran, *Biblical Prophets in Byzantine Palestine: Reassessing the Lives of the Prophets* (New York: Brill, 1995) 110.

[5]Smith, *To Take Place*, 89.

of the authors is that the gospel be preached more fully—that the words of Jesus may be grounded in a specific place and time so as to speak more genuinely in this place and time. To picture the historical world and geography of Jesus is to allow ourselves to enter more fully into the mystery of the story, to "re-member" ourselves among those early hearers, and to feel the presence of the holy in those ancient words spoken long ago in a real place.

Part One introduces the reader to the biblical concept of sacred space and a theology of the land drawn from both the Old and New Testaments. This section serves to ground the person of faith, whether he or she has visited Israel/Palestine or not, in the theological framework of "Holy Land." Part Two places each of the Sunday gospels in a particular locale within Israel/Palestine. Using Cycle A as the primary Gospel, the location of Jesus is traced from the First Week of Advent through Ordinary Time, Lent and Easter. The synoptic Gospels follow a somewhat similar pattern, so that the readings of Cycles B and C adhere closely to those of Cycle A. However, where a Gospel writer has introduced a different setting, that place is interjected into the Cycle A pattern. In other words, in Cycle A, the Tenth Sunday of Ordinary Time places Jesus in Capernaum; however, that same Sunday in Cycle C has him in Nain. In such cases, Cycle A appears first, followed by Cycle C.

In some instances, the Gospel writers place the same story in different locations. For example, Matthew tells of Jesus' "Sermon on the Mount," while Luke places Jesus on a plain. If such differences reflect the Gospel writer's theology and are not related to a specific space, the site currently revered is used. The Good Friday readings include several locations. Because of the significance of these events, the readings are listed under the various sites at which the events occurred.

The greatest problem in such an undertaking is that in most cases the sites reverenced are not necessarily the "actual" location. The land of Palestine shortly after the experience of Jesus was ravaged by war. The Romans destroyed Jerusalem in 70 C.E.,[6] and in the years following the final destruction much of Galilee and Judea was ravaged. The sites recognized today as holy, in most cases, were originally named so by Byzantine Christians on pilgrimage in the fourth to the seventh centuries. The general area is accurate; the specific location unknown. The skeptic may say, "So why photograph it?" As Chapter One will explain, what is sacred and what is held holy are not always determined by the act that occurred on a particular spot but by the remembering of that act by the faithful who believed this or that to be the location.

---

[6]Whenever dates occur before the Common Era, they will be designated B.C.E. (formerly B.C.). All other dates are from the Common Era (formerly A.D.).

Always taken into consideration are relative distances. The Sea of Galilee is about thirteen miles long and seven miles wide. One can easily see across it. The towns and villages of Jesus' day were never too far from one another. Capernaum, Magdala, Nain, Cana, Nazareth—all were within twenty miles of one another.

The landscape photographed and the reflections on the sites paint a geography little changed since the time of Jesus and his followers. To see the Judean Wilderness or the River Jordan or the hills of Jerusalem is to see the topography, the land features that existed two thousand years ago. And in seeing them, we are reminded that this is what Jesus saw. The dust and heat are the realities of his day and time as much as they are ours. So, in a very real way, to encounter the land, if only through word and image, is to touch the world of Jesus and, we believe, in some small way to touch the divine.

The authors would like to thank their religious congregations, the Sisters of St. Joseph of LaGrange and the Sinsinawa Dominicans, for providing the opportunity to study the Bible in the land of its inspiration. The faculty of Biblical Literature and Languages at Catholic Theological Union in Chicago, particularly Barbara Bowe, R.S.C.J., Carolyn Osiek, R.S.C.J., and Barbara Reid, O.P., provided both support and critique in the writing process. In addition, the faculty of the Religious Studies Department and the students at Dominican University, River Forest, Illinois, lent encouragement throughout the development of *In This Place.*

Also, helpful were Janet Ewens, O.P., Therese Middendorf, C.S.J., Elizabeth Pawlicki, O.P., and Michelle Vanderbilt, O.P., for their willingness to read, pray, and critically review this work. Virginia Stone, B.V.M., suggested the title for the book. Rev. Steve Gavit's assistance in Israel made the photography possible. Maryann Tamasauskas's love of the land, particularly the desert of Judea, opened up the possibility of metaphor and symbol out of the wilderness of arid sand.

Dr. Kenneth Holum of the University of Maryland and Dr. Abner Raban and Yael Arnon of Haifa University assisted in interpreting the archaeology of Israel.

Much of the inspiration for this publication has come from the participants of the Israel Study Program at Catholic Theological Union, Chicago. Their enthusiasm for the Land encouraged us to create a work that would integrate experience of the land and culture with the events of the Gospels.

Chapter One

What Makes the Land Holy?

Living, even briefly, in Israel/Palestine brings one into close contact with Middle Eastern and Mediterranean cultures. The visitor, especially a Westerner, will be surrounded by different dress, strange foods, the smell of unnamed spices, a variety of languages, and even unusual modes of transportation. A man on a donkey in the midst of frightful traffic is not an uncommon sight in East Jerusalem. A particularly disarming feature for some is the ease and frequency of public prayer, or at least the visible trappings of religion for both the Jew and the Muslim. For some it is this conscious religious dimension that brings about a gradual, growing awareness of a sense of the sacred in the local people that is quite different from the secular tone of most Western societies.

The cultural difference here is deep. The sense of the sacred we see lived in the religious peoples of the Middle East is a hint of the "cosmic religiosity" that French philosopher Mircea Eliade describes as the type of religious experience that dominated the world before Judaism and is still present in some primitive Asiatic societies.[1] In these societies a religious experience is not something rational or speculative. It is not an idea, abstraction, or moral allegory. A religious experience, a hierophany, is an experience of awe-inspiring mystery or of majesty emanating from a power that is wholly other than human. Moses had an experience like that while tending his father-in-law's flocks on Mount Horeb.

> There an angel of the LORD appeared to him in fire flaming out of a bush. As he looked on, he was surprised to see that the bush, though on fire, was not consumed. So Moses decided, "I must go over to look at this remarkable sight, and see why the bush is not burned." When the LORD saw him coming over to look at it more

---

[1] Wendell Beane and William Doty, eds., *Myths, Rites, Symbols: A Mircea Eliade Reader* (New York: Harper, 1975) 128.

1

closely, God called out to him from the bush, "Moses! Moses!" He answered, "Here I am." God said, "Come no nearer! Remove the sandals from your feet, for the place where you stand is holy ground" (Exod 3:2-6).

Eliade would define Moses' experience in the following way: "Something sacred shows itself to us, something of a wholly different order, a reality that does not belong to our world, in an object that is an integral part of our world."[2] There is paradox in this definition. The manifestation of the sacred, that is, something beyond this world, shows itself in or through an object that is of this world. The object, such as the burning bush on Mount Horeb, remains itself yet at the same time becomes something else. For the religious person, a "burning bush" experience is a break or interruption in the world in which we live, revealing the sacred. For Moses, the burning bush was not only a hierophany but a theophany, an experience of God. This kind of experience can be so significant that the "break in space" becomes a fixed point or central axis for future reference. Moses' encounter with God at the burning bush on Mount Horeb became the reference point that gave direction to the rest of his life. Moses was incredulous that God could possibly expect him to lead the Israelites out of Egypt to a new land. Yet the story of the Israelites' journey and our covenant history begins with this moment.

A sacred place, such as Mount Horeb, is a place where transcendence is possible. The mountain image as a place of transcendence is a common one. Many other societies have a sacred mountain or "high place." Mountains are the nearest thing to the sky. Their vertical shape suggests transcendence. The mountaintop is the place where sky and earth meet; thus it is the "dwelling place of the gods." For example, Mount Meru is a mythical mountain that has "centered" the world of the majority of Asians who follow the beliefs of the Hindu, Buddhist, and Jain religions. Above Meru stands the polestar. Daily the Sun drives his chariot around the mountain. The heavenly Ganges, in its descent to earth, first touches Meru and then divides into four rivers that run in the four cardinal directions to water the earth.[3] In Iran, Mount Hara Berezaiti has a central place in the Zoroastrian tradition. It is the pivot around which the sun and stars revolve. In Japan, Mount Fuji is thought to link heaven and earth. In Sri Lanka, there is an indentation on Adam's Peak that is believed to be the footprint of

---

[2] Mircea Eliade, *The Sacred and the Profane* (New York: Harper & Row, 1959) 11.

[3] Diana L. Eck, "Mountains," *The Encyclopedia of Religion*, ed. Mircea Eliade (New York: Macmillan, 1987) 10:130–131.

Buddha, Siva, Adam, or the Apostle Thomas, depending on one's religious affiliation—Buddhist, Hindu, Moslem, or Christian respectively.

Ascending a mountain is associated with gaining a new vision or increasing in spiritual insight. Thus, transformation is part of the mountain experience. Mount Hira near Mecca is the place where Mohammed heard the revealed word of the Qurʾan. Moses was transformed into the leader of the Israelites on Mount Sinai, and through him the Israelites became covenanted people on this sacred mountain. Jesus was transfigured on a mountain in Galilee. The significance of "mountain"—its shape, height, and the experience of ascent—in humankind's search for and communication with the sacred is reflected in the architecture of places of worship. Temple, church, pagoda, and pyramid stretch toward the sky in a vertical passageway to the divine. It is safe to say that the mountain is a universal symbol of a physical, tangible way that leads humankind as close to God (or the gods) as possible.

In the history of the world's religions, another common concept is the naming of a specific place as "the center of the world." There are several specific locations in the world today that some society at some time in history has considered to be "the navel of the world." What is important about these places for this discussion is the significant event that brought about this designation and the behavior of the people toward their "center." In Greek mythology it is said that Zeus set two eagles loose from opposite ends of the earth. The spot below where they met was the center or navel of the world. It was marked with a special stone called an *omphalos* (the Greek word for "navel") and was named Delphi. For one thousand years Delphi was considered the holiest place in Greece.[4] There was, until the fourth century, an oracle at Delphi visited by people from all over Greece and beyond. The oracle of Apollo at Delphi was questioned by individuals about business, marriage, farming, and other enterprises. This oracle was also visited by such notables as Alexander the Great and Nero, the emperor of Rome. The setting of Delphi amidst the peaks of the Mount Parnassus range is spectacular.

In Norse mythology, Himinbjorg lies at the center of the earth. Here the rainbow touches the vault of heaven. In Mecca the Kaʾbah is revered by Muslims as the center of the world. The Kaʾbah is a stone structure in the center of the Grand Mosque of Mecca. It is toward the Kaʾbah that Muslims orient themselves in prayer; thus it is a spiritual center. The Kaʾbah is the focal point of the Hajj, the pilgrimage that is one of the five pillars of Islam. Near the ancient city of Shechem (current-day

[4] James Harpur, *The Atlas of Sacred Places* (New York: Henry Holt, 1994) 194.

Nablus) in Palestine lies Mount Gerizim. Judges 9:37 describes Gerizim as the *omphalos tēs gēs*,[5] "the navel of the earth." The territory that surrounds Mount Gerizim was considered consecrated by those who lived and worshiped near it. From the Syrian *Book of the Cave Treasures*,[6] a Christian tradition describes Golgotha as the center of the world and the culmination of salvation. Here Adam was created and buried; here Christ died and rose. Indeed, in the Church of the Holy Sepulcher in Jerusalem, before recent renovations removed it, a white marble hemisphere in the Greek choir marked the ground beneath this church as the center of the Christian world.

Throughout the world, in virtually every culture, humankind has located and named some specific place or places as "sacred space." Whatever the religious conceptions are or the images used to express them, the experience of the sacred (or the memory of that experience) and its consequent determining effect on the society follow a similar pattern. The sequence has four parts.[7] First there is the "breakthrough in space," a breaking in or irruption of the sacred, which is experienced by a specific person in the society at a specific place. The place is chosen by God; it cannot be determined from the worldly side. Second, the experience of the "break in space" includes some symbol or image of an opening by which passage from one cosmic plane to another is possible. Third, through this opening some communication with heaven occurs, represented by an image such as a ladder or pillar, which then becomes the *axis mundi*, the "center of the world." Finally, around this "center" lies the world in which the people live,[8] that is, from their experience of the sacred the system of their world is defined. Beyond their "world" is chaos, uninhabitable by human beings because it is a place where communication with the supernatural world is impossible. In the "other world" dwell demons, monsters, and foreigners.

This center then becomes the heart of reality, the place where the individual recognizes his or her own spiritual identity and is drawn into the collective spiritual destiny of all humankind who share this center. With this definition of sacred space and center of the world, clearly it is possible to have multiple "centers," because each space defines a special relationship to the divine. This description of "center" also pro-

---

[5] Jeffrey K. Lott, "Gerizim," *Anchor Bible Dictionary,* ed. Noel Freedman (New York: Doubleday, 1992) 2:993.

[6] Mircea Eliade and Lawrence E. Sullivan, "Center of the World," *The Encyclopedia of Religion,* ed. Mircea Eliade (New York: Macmillan, 1987) 3:166–174.

[7] See Mircea Eliade, *The Sacred and the Profane,* 20–29.

[8] Ibid., 37.

vides some explanation for why many Christians who go to Jerusalem are seeing the place for the first time yet have a strong feeling of being "at home."

A familiar biblical story provides a good example of sacred space. Jacob's dream is the context of his religious experience and the ladder an image that describes both this passageway and the communication it provides.

> Jacob departed from Beer-sheba and proceeded toward Haran. When he came upon a certain shrine, as the sun had already set, he stopped there for the night. Taking one of the stones at the shrine, he put it under his head and lay down to sleep at that spot. Then he had a dream: a stairway rested on the ground, with its top reaching to the heavens; and God's messengers were going up and down on it. And there was the LORD standing beside him and saying: "I, the LORD, am the God of your forefather Abraham and the God of Isaac; the land on which you are lying I will give to you and your descendants. These shall be as plentiful as the dust of the earth, and through them you shall spread out east and west, north and south. In you and your descendants all the nations of the earth shall find blessing. Know that I am with you; I will protect you wherever you go, and bring you back to this land. I will never leave you until I have done what I promised you."
>
> When Jacob awoke from his sleep, he exclaimed, "Truly, the LORD is in this spot, although I did not know it!" In solemn wonder he cried out: "How awesome is this shrine! This is nothing else but an abode of God, and that is the gateway to heaven!" Early the next morning Jacob took the stone that he had put under his head, set it up as a memorial stone, and poured oil on top of it. He called that site Bethel . . . (Gen 28:10-19).

Jacob's experience contains the four elements described above. He has come to the end of a day's journey; he pitches camp for the night, falls asleep, and has a dream. At the beginning of the story the place does not have a name; it is "toward Haran." The choice of this place to stop for the night was accidental; Jacob did not go there to have a religious experience. While asleep, Jacob has an extraordinary dream. In his dream he "sees" a passage to a plane beyond this world. The image used to describe the passageway is "a stairway [that] rested on the ground, with its top reaching to the heavens." An image something like this is found in the story of the tower of Babel (Gen 11:1-9). The people attempt to build a tower that will reach into the heavens. The result is confusion of language and the people are scattered. The first principle of sacred place has been violated in this account. One cannot choose the place where the sacred will break in.

The message given to Jacob from God is about the land to be given to Jacob and his descendants: "the land on which you are lying I will give to you and your descendants." From this location Jacob's descendants shall spread out east and west, north and south. When he wakes up, Jacob's "pillow" becomes a "pillar," a sacred stone, often a symbol found at ancient sanctuaries. He pours oil on it, thus anointing it, that is, marking it as holy and set aside for God. The place is named Bethel, meaning "house of God," and becomes a "center" from which the people of Israel will grow. Bethel, about fourteen miles north of Jerusalem, remained a northern sanctuary until destroyed about 621 B.C.E. by King Josiah's attempt to centralize worship in Jerusalem (2 Kgs 23:15).

The idea or sense of sacred space is not a common one in modern Western society, except perhaps for the interior of a church. The church building is a different space than the street outside. The doorway or threshold provides a boundary that distinguishes two worlds, the profane and the religious. The threshold is also the place where the two worlds communicate; it provides the possibility of passage from the profane to the sacred. Thresholds are both symbolic of the "break in space" where the sacred touches our world and also the vehicle by which one may pass into communication with the sacred.

Many cultures and religions recognize the significance of the threshold with a variety of rituals. In the Catholic Church holy water is placed at the entrance to the church as a reminder of the cleansing of baptism and the preparation this cleansing provides for the worshiper to participate in the holy mysteries. Muslims wash thoroughly before prayer and remove their shoes before entering the mosque. At the domestic threshold, a bow, prostration, or handshake may take place before entering the house. At the entrance to the Treasury of Pharaoh, the tomb of a Nabatean king and the most photographed of the ancient monuments at Petra, there is a large bowl-like indentation. This indentation was needed to gather the blood of the animal sacrifice offered at the threshold to please or appease the guardian divinities. In ancient cities in Israel and Egypt, the city gates, threshold to the community inside, provided the place for judgment. Here, too, in the example of the rituals surrounding the threshold found in so many different cultures, one can recognize a common gesture full of meaning throughout the history of humankind.

Western culture could benefit by recognizing the significance of sacred space in other cultures. We often turn a blind eye to the "holy" in our midst. Other than a holy water fountain inside the church door and the almost extinct gesture of carrying one's bride through the doorway of the couple's first dwelling, the significance of threshold is lost on us. Difficult too, particularly for white North Americans, is the ability to experience the holy, whether in another faith's "sacred place" or in our own land. Though there is in our society the same longing to encounter God, we have, as Annie Dillard says, "doused the burning bush and cannot rekindle it; we are lighting matches in vain under every green tree."[9]

The Western mind has been diverted for perhaps thousands of years from a natural sense of the sacred as manifested in nature and matter itself. Recognizing the sacred in the objects around us is *a way of being in the world.* Several scholars suggest that the Judeo-Christian tradition has diminished our connections between God and the natural environment.[10] The roots of our being disenfranchised from the holy in our natural world can be traced to Baʿal. As discussed earlier, people have tended to choose high places for their worship, an exposed site where the "god" was likely to see what they were doing. There they would perform some act comparable to what they wished their god to do for them. Baʿal was the most significant god in the Canaanite pantheon and was the presiding deity in many localities. Baʿal was also worshiped on high places in Moab in the time of Balaam and Balak (Num 22:41). In the period of the Judges there were altars to Baʿal in Palestine (Judg 2:13; 6:28-32); and in the time of Ahab and Jezebel, the worship of the Israelite God was almost supplanted by that of Baʿal.

The struggle Israel experienced transforming the land of Canaan into the Promised Land of Israel included a fierce competition between Yahweh and Baʿal. In Exodus 34:13, Canaanite altars are described as having a sacred pole and stone pillars, which the Israelites are to destroy. Before they enter Canaan, Yahweh gives these strict instructions to Moses: "Tell the Israelites: When you go across the Jordan into the land of Canaan, drive out all the inhabitants of the land before you; destroy all their stone figures and molten images, and demolish all their high places" (Num 33:51-52). In Deuteronomy the Israelites receive instructions on how *not* to build an altar: "You shall not plant a sacred pole of any kind of wood beside the altar of the LORD, your God, which you will build; nor shall you erect a sacred pillar, such as the LORD, your God, detests" (Deut 16:21-22). In other words, be sure that the Israelite rituals and places of worship can be distinguished from those used to worship other gods.

---

[9] Annie Dillard, *Teaching a Stone to Talk* (New York: Harper & Row, 1982) 70.

[10] Belden Lane, *Landscapes of the Sacred* (Mahwah, N.J.: Paulist Press, 1988); Wendell Beane and William Doty, eds., *Myths, Rites, Symbols: A Mircea Eliade Reader,* vols. 1–2 (New York: Harper & Row, 1975); Walter Brueggemann, *The Land* (Philadelphia: Fortress, 1977) are three authors who support this idea.

The worship of Baʿal was marked chiefly by fertility rites. The main function of Baʿal was to make land, animals and people fertile. Worship tended to be "earthy," using objects the worshipers hoped would flourish. This makes sense in an agricultural society dependent on crops and animals, but to the Israelites this was a false, earthbound deity. The God of Israel was a transcendent God of history, not encumbered by the natural environment. The destruction of the high places and anything that smacked of Canaanite worship led to a "disenchantment" with the world.[11] Judaism, and later Christianity, focused religious practices away from nature. Again it is Mircea Eliade who says, "It was the prophets, apostles and their successors, the missionaries, who convinced the Western world that a rock (which certain people considered to be sacred) was only a rock, that the planets and stars were only cosmic objects, that is to say, that they were not (and could not be) either gods or angels or demons. It is as a result of this long process of desacralization of nature that the Westerner has managed to *see a natural object* where our ancestors saw a sacred presence."[12]

In addition to this suspicion of nature, developments in philosophy and psychology through thinkers like Marx, Nietzsche, and Freud have influenced our culture and given us a sense of power in our own autonomy. This positive affirmation of the human intellect and psyche doesn't fit with an interpretation of scriptural language that would have us completely dependent on a Higher Being. "We conceive ourselves as authors of our own meaning and being, set in the midst of a world there for us to interrogate, manipulate, and control."[13] The German philosopher Ludwig Feuerbach (1804–1872) is called the father of atheism. He taught that by using religious language to explain self and existence, we "empty our human substance into an illusory absolute."[14] These nineteenth-century developments in philosophy, theology, and psychology have had a monumental influence on the basic life assumptions that undergird Western society.

The abundant scholarly work accomplished in the area of biblical criticism by sociologists, anthropologists, and archaeologists in the last century has dissected biblical texts and challenged much of the traditional or literal understanding that has been the basis for our faith life. All these aspects of our modern culture have distanced us from a sense of the sacred in our lives.

[11] Lane, *Landscapes of the Sacred*, 18.

[12] Beane, *Myths*, 128.

[13] Paul Ricoeur, *Essays on Biblical Interpretation*, ed. Lewis Mudge (Philadelphia: Fortress, 1980) 4.

[14] Ibid., 5.

The faithful pilgrim may come to the Holy Land seeking an experience of the sacred, only to discover many of his or her biblical stories unmasked as myth. A fear that beyond the literal is only confusion or emotion creates a barrier to scriptural language with its metaphors, visions, and parables. How can we avoid this emptiness and recover meaning from symbol? Logic, critical analysis, and the advances of science and technology do not render us incapable of responding to the sacred. "Beyond the desert of criticism, we wish to be called again," says the French philosopher Paul Ricoeur.[15] He suggests that our contemporary culture has become insensitive to the experience of God and the signs of the sacred that surround us. We do not see ourselves as belonging to the sacred. We need to be summoned to the biblical message again, to its springs of water for the thirsty spirit. The Holy Land and all its holy places will, potentially, flood the visitor with these springs of water.

However, a lack of ease with "symbol" may be a barrier that blocks a connection between the land, the place, and the heart of the visitor. Ricoeur has constructed a theory of interpretation of meaning from symbol that will help us move beyond our demythologized state to a "second naiveté." The stories of Moses seeing and recognizing as "holy ground" the place of the burning bush on Mount Horeb and of Jacob creating a sanctuary at Bethel after his vision of angels ascending and descending are stories from a time and culture that could be called a "first naiveté." The "break in space," as Eliade calls it, that Moses and Jacob experienced, would go unquestioned by them as anything other than a communication "of the gods," that is, from beyond this world; that was the only possible explanation. Their world was a world in which symbol came naturally.

Though that seems impossible for us today, we still need the meaning the symbol gives to us. "The symbol gives rise to thought" is the philosopher's way of saying it.[16] For Ricoeur, this does not mean that the symbol in some way expresses my life, but that the symbol *makes me think.* We cannot go back and live the symbolism with Moses and Jacob, but we can aim at a "second naiveté" through criticism and interpretation. The symbol's gift of meaning and our effort to understand it are knotted together in a paradox. We must understand in order to believe, but we must believe in order to understand. Put another way, Ricoeur says, "Never does the interpreter get near to what his text says unless he lives in the aura of the meaning he is inquiring after."[17]

[15] Paul Ricoeur, *The Symbolism of Evil* (New York: Harper & Row, 1967) 349.
[16] Ibid., 347–357.
[17] Ibid., 351.

To demythologize is to separate by critical method the historical from the pseudo-historical. But in this process of intellectual honesty and objectivity, the dimension of the text or symbol as a sign of the sacred is brought to light. And so, Ricoeur goes on to say, the dissolution of the myth as explanation is the necessary way to the restoration of the myth as symbol. The literal interpretation of myth may be suspended, but its symbolic meaning is affirmed. Achieving this distinction is to arrive at a "second naiveté," which Ricoeur declares, "aims to be the post-critical equivalent of the precritical hierophany."[18]

A good example of the Ricoeur process can be found in *The Holy Land*, a guidebook for Israel/Palestine. Author Jerome Murphy-O'Connor, O.P., comments on the potential for disillusionment at one's first experience of the Church of the Holy Sepulcher in Jerusalem:

> One expects the central shrine of Christendom to stand out in majestic isolation, but anonymous buildings cling to it like barnacles. One looks for numinous light, but it is dark and cramped. One hopes for peace, but the ear is assailed by a cacophony of warring chants. One desires holiness, only to encounter a jealous possessiveness: the six groups of occupants—Latin Catholics, Greek Orthodox, Armenians, Syrians, Copts, Ethiopians—watch one another suspiciously for any infringement of rights. The frailty of humanity is nowhere more apparent than here; it epitomizes the human condition. The empty who come to be filled will leave desolate; *those who permit the church to question them* [emphasis added] may begin to understand why hundreds of thousands thought it worthwhile to risk death or slavery in order to pray here.[19]

What questions might the Church of the Holy Sepulcher raise for the faithful Christian? Recalling the significant events remembered here, one is confronted with his or her own beliefs about the resurrection of Jesus. How does what I believe about the resurrection affect my faith life? What have Christians throughout the ages thought about the resurrection? Do the daily chaos and diversity found within this church building somehow symbolize the ambiguity and contradiction surrounding the question of the historicity of the resurrection within Church tradition? These are just a few of the considerations that could arise for "those who allow the church to question them."

In the same way *the land* of Israel/Palestine, with its familiar names such as Jerusalem, Jericho, Nazareth, Bethlehem, and Capernaum and

---

[18] Ibid., 352.

[19] Jerome Murphy-O'Connor, O.P., *The Holy Land* (New York: Oxford University Press, 1992) 49.

places like the Mount of Olives, the Judean hills, the Sea of Galilee, shapes our understanding of the events that happened here. The land speaks, the land questions, the land informs. We need to know the geography, with its climate, topography, and history, to better understand the symbols, myths, and legends woven throughout our tradition and the texts of Scripture. We need the fullness of language, the whole range of tradition and Scriptural expression, to stimulate the questions, to generate the experience in us, to find ourselves and give meaning to our life's experiences.

What makes the Holy Land holy? What makes one's experience of the land an encounter with holiness? Several elements might be considered. The centrality of the land promise for Judaism marks Old Testament sites as holy. The Incarnation and subsequent transformation of the land promise into the fullness of life in Christ distinguishes New Testament geography as touched by God. The origin and history of the term "holy land" in the Christian tradition reminds us of the land made holy by the feet of pilgrims. A review of sacred space as it is reverenced in a variety of cultures suggests both a common longing for, and a common experience of, the transcendent throughout history. Philosophers such as Paul Ricoeur propose a process that moves the individual believer from the encounter with myth and symbol to a deeper understanding of her or his own faith story. All these elements are pieces of what makes "the land" and one's experience of it holy. There is one more piece.

One could travel throughout the Holy Land of Israel, Jordan, Egypt, Greece, and Turkey from one fabulous site to another: the Acropolis, Ephesus, the Holy Sepulcher, Galilee, Sinai, Petra, Giza, Karnak, and more. Any one of these places could provide enough history, information, symbol, myth, and religious experience for a lifetime of reflection. But it is possible to stand on the "holy ground" and have no relationship with it. To have some affinity with the place means being in some way part of a communal experience. Whether one goes as a tourist, pilgrim, or student, as an individual or with a group, one does not experience these places alone. Part of perceiving the holiness of a place is knowing something of the community whose story tells of its sacredness. If the site is a Christian one, then being with a community whose members share this common faith will be an integral part of the experience.

Belden Lane, in his book *Landscapes of the Sacred*, presents as his thesis for this particular work that "the experiences of place profoundly structure our experience of self and others in relationship to God. . . . Conversely, our spirituality structures our 'landscape,' that is, our vision of the 'where' of our experience."[20] Lane uses a quote from Ortega

---

[20] Lane, *Landscapes of the Sacred*, xi.

y Gasset to introduce his hermeneutics of landscape: "Tell me the landscape in which you live and I will tell you who you are." It is the concept behind Gasset's words that have prompted the writing of this book.

All of us have our own sacred places—places significant because of personal or family connections, retreat, vacations, liturgical or prayer events, history, or culture. The geography of these places has shaped us and our relationship with God. So, too, did the geography of the Holy Land shape Jesus. He grew up in a small town; his public ministry was in the modest villages and open spaces of Galilee. The examples he used in preaching were drawn from the daily lives and work of the people he knew. The message we hear in the gospels today will be enhanced by a familiarity with the shape of the landscape. How did the availability of lonely places to pray, the proximity of desert to city, familiarity with a sea that could be transformed from calm to tempestuous in minutes, the experience of pilgrimage to Jerusalem for Jewish festival celebrations, etc., contribute to Jesus' understanding of himself and others in relationship to God?

Another title for this book might have been *How Geography Shaped the Gospels*. For those who have never experienced the holy places of Judaism and the origins of Christianity, it is our hope that the descriptions which follow will "transport" you to the "place" where the event happened. For those who have encountered this land, may this book lead you to new insights rendered by the landscape itself.

Chapter 2

A Theology of the Land of the Bible

To hike the rocky snake path up Mount Sinai, to sit on the Mount of Olives overlooking the Old City of Jerusalem, to stand in a dark corner of the Holy Sepulcher—to touch holy ground is for some to touch the Divine. Because as Christians we believe in the inbreaking experience of the Incarnation, that Jesus became God's Son—tangible, human, in history—we are quick to search for the sacred in our surroundings. We hope to touch a part of the mystery of God, to feel the spirit anew, to have our faith bolstered by the real.

This very human desire to find God in our world impels a theology of the land, a theology ancient and rich. The very first act recorded in the Bible is the creation of the earth, and one of the last images in the Bible is that of "a new heaven and a new earth." The Christian Scriptures, then, are rooted in this sense of earthiness, grounded in specificality. God acts in history. But God also acts in particular places. The how and where of God's actions were often troubling for the Israelites and early followers of Jesus. The God who gifted with promises of land is also the God who exiles.

The Old Testament presents several ways of looking at the land: as gift, as promise, as inheritance, as punishment. The New Testament, written for the most part outside the "land of Israel," presents a development of land theology that challenges some of what precedes it in the Hebrew Scriptures. Both affect how the faithful hear and understand the Scriptures today in places most often far removed from the Holy Land. Understanding some of what shaped those developing theologies allows the reader to see the significance place and locality can play in our Sunday gospels.

Land Theology in the Old Testament

Israel's relationship to the land is inseparable from its relationship with God. Some scholars would claim that the land theme is the central motif in the Old Testament.[1] The Book of Genesis begins with God's creation of the earth (*'eres*) and the human creature formed from the "clay of the ground" (*adama*: Gen 2:7). From the beginning of this relationship, humankind is close to the soil and is entrusted with the stewardship of this gift.

Adam and Eve are sent out of the garden (Gen 3:22); Cain becomes a wanderer after killing his brother (Gen 4:8); Noah and a few others are the only ones to survive the flood (Gen 6:5ff.); the Tower of Babel scatters the people over the face of the earth (Gen 11:1ff.). In each of these narratives the sequence of humankind's action and God's consequent judgment results in a loss of the land. Thus, in the history of the creation (Gen 1–11) a theology is presented in which land is God's gift. It is humankind's "divine destiny to fill the world and possess their land."[2] Their task is to care for the land within some limits set by God (see Gen 2:15-17), while always acknowledging the land as gift.

Humankind, however, has ownership tendencies. The stories of Adam and Eve, Cain, and others show either the failure to follow God's rules regarding the land or an assumption of ownership of the land excluding a partnership with God. It is this desire to be autonomous that brings on God's judgment, resulting in the people's loss of land and a consequent experience of great vulnerability. But the relationship is not ended by this failure. The ordeal of landlessness or "wilderness" becomes, paradoxically, "the context for the greatest experience of God's grace."[3] We all have this wilderness experience in our own faith journey. A loss or separation leads to disillusionment about God in our lives, yet becomes the setting for a new and deeper relationship. For Israel, the land promise survives the crisis and continues as the underlying motif throughout the Old Testament. Indeed, the promise made to Abraham (Gen 12:1) follows immediately after the Adam and Eve story, thus restoring hope to a people who have just been evicted from the land.

There are two Hebrew words frequently used in the Bible that translate as "land." The first and most common is *'eres*, meaning "earth," "ground," or, alternately, "country." *'Eres* is translated as "land" when referring to a specific geographic region (e.g., "land of Ararat": 2 Kgs 19:37) or to an area belonging to a specific group (e.g., "land of the

---

[1] W. Janzen, "Land," *Anchor Bible Dictionary*, ed. David Freedman (New York: Doubleday, 1992) 4:143–154.

[2] Richard J. Clifford, "Genesis," *New Jerome Biblical Commentary*, ed. Raymond E. Brown, Joseph A. Fitzmyer, Roland E. Murphy (Englewood Cliffs, N.J.: Prentice Hall, 1990) 9.

[3] Janzen, *Anchor Bible Dictionary*, 4:146.

Kenites, Kenizzites, etc.: Gen 15:19). *ʾEres* is often used in a context that indicates the land is possessed or claimed by Israel or promised to it (Deut 34:2: "land of Judah"). *Adama* is the other Hebrew word that translates as "land." *Adama* can also mean "country" or "soil." It does not have the political implications suggested by *ʾeres* but instead refers to agricultural land, i.e., land that sustains a population. ("He will love and bless and multiply you; he will bless the fruit of your womb and the produce of your *soil* . . .": Deut 7:13). *Adama* may be owned by an individual or group, but God's ultimate ownership is assumed (Isa 14:2; Hos 9:3).[4]

As the story of Israel unfolds in Deuteronomistic history, the specific and consistent contextual references to "land" have significant implications. That *ʾeres* refers to a certain geographic region or belonging to a distinctive people is an indication that God's relationship with God's people is expressed, lived out in a particular place. Possession of that place in a political manner is part of God's promise. The place will be sufficiently rich agriculturally *(adama)* to sustain God's people, however numerous they become. God is always in charge. The right to the land is a God-given right, but this right will be forfeited if the people violate the law for the land. These descriptions and expectations provide the framework for a land theology.

In his work on this topic, Walter Brueggemann uses the "land" theme as a prism of biblical faith. Israel's faith is a journeying in and out of the land. Brueggemann's approach has an important significance relative to the experience of those who have spent time in Israel. As the land of Israel is explored and concrete places are identified as meaningful in the faith life of the Israelite community, we begin to perceive concrete events that have formed our own faith. Brueggemann stays within the limits of other scholars' work on biblical history and does not reduce Israel's past to myth, yet he tells the story in a way that has an effect on our own consciousness. Israel's faith journey becomes our own history and destiny as a faith community.

The desire for land, a particular place one calls home, is a response to the human hunger for belonging. Throughout our world today one finds hundreds of thousands of refugees, people who have been displaced from their homeland because of war, political oppression, famine, or natural disaster. The images cast on our TV screens and other news media show men, women, and children living in crowded situations, deplorable health conditions, without sufficient food, water, clothing, shelter, or medical support. Their faces are images of hopelessness and despair. In our own cities homelessness is increasing

---

[4] Ibid., 4:143–144.

to critical proportions. The exodus from Egypt, the wandering in the desert, the exile to Babylon recorded in the Bible are realities of daily life for many in our world today. Besides those who are literally without a home or homeland, there are many in our society, including ourselves from time to time, who feel lost, disoriented, or without roots. The loss of actual turf or a sense of rootlessness is an experience all of us share with our ancestors in the faith.

Israel yearned for a homeland, a place where their feet could be planted, a place where they could reside "with Yahweh." There they would be secure as Yahweh's chosen people. This homeland would not only sustain them with its agricultural produce but also with its beauty. Recognizing its beauty and enjoying the land would be possible because of the security and freedom they would experience in a land entrusted to them. This homeland would be where family and friends would gather to worship, work, grow, love, and play. Here family events would take place and the community would be formed. Memories created in this land would become the identity of the people and provide continuity across generations. For Israel, land as described above was part of God's promise. Whether it be the garden in Genesis 2:15-17 or the land toward which Abraham sets out in Genesis 12:1, a homeland would be a place where Israel could be prosperous and continue its intimate friendship with Yahweh.

The ancestral narratives in Genesis 12–50 begin with Abraham and all his household moving "to a land that I will show you" (Gen 12:1). Yahweh has required something quite radical. To comply means to leave the known in search of the unknown, to rely on Yahweh for everything. This movement, which lasted through the generations of Abraham, Isaac, and Jacob, is freely chosen and full of hope. God's promise of a better place provides courage and stamina for the journey.

Bruggemann uses three specific images of Israel as both a landed and a landless people in his development of land theology. Abraham and his followers accept landlessness and become *sojourners*. To be a sojourner is to be on the way, yearning for a homeland, living as an outsider. The term means "resident alien," i.e., being *in* a place but not *of* the place. A sojourner never really belongs to a place as one with rights or decision-making privilege. Life as a sojourner requires a certain posture of faith. It means knowing that this place is not, finally, where one belongs. It means waiting in hope, not knowing how, when or where the promise of a "better place" will be fulfilled.

Israel's image and memory of itself after the slavery of Egypt are that of *wanderer*. Israel is in the wilderness, without resources, focusing all its energy on survival. There is no progress in wandering. It is more a state of being than a movement toward something. Desert wilderness is a place to die. Israel's image of Yahweh's promise of a "better place" grows dim. The Israelites are still landless and the journey isn't romantic anymore. The community becomes restless and angry. Yahweh is still with Israel, but they doubt the promise (Deut 1:32). Without faith or a homeland, Israel is wandering without a sense of direction. These sentiments of the wanderer are captured by the psalmist in Psalm 106:21-24:

> They forgot the God who saved them,
>> who did great deeds in Egypt. . . .
> Next they despised the beautiful land;
>> they did not believe the promise.

The third image of Israel as a landless people occurs during their periods of *exile*. In both Assyria (eighth century B.C.E.) and Babylon (sixth century B.C.E.), Israel was alienated from that which gave identity: the land. Loss of identity meant loss of continuity with the tradition. Whether one is oppressed or not in a period of exile, one has become detached from the roots that give life and strength. One's traditions and rituals have less meaning and become a memory of another time and another place. Again, it is the psalmist who expresses best what it is like to be in exile:

> By the rivers of Babylon
>> we sat mourning and weeping
>> when we remembered Zion.
> On the poplars of that land
>> we hung up our harps,
> There our captors asked us
>> for the words of a song;
> Our tormentors, for a joyful song:
>> "Sing for us a song of Zion!"
> But how could we sing a song of the LORD
>> in a foreign land?
> If I forget you, Jerusalem,
>> may my right hand wither.
> May my tongue stick to my palate
>> if I do not remember you . . . (Ps 137:1-6).

The task in a time of exile is to keep the memory alive, to adjust, perhaps even to settle in, but never to lose sight of God's promise. Paradoxically, it is in exile that Israel's hope of return to the land, though they see no way for this to happen, transforms and renews their memory of the covenant. In Jeremiah we read that with God's "age-old love" (Jer 31:3), Israel's repentance (Jer 31:18-19), and God's forgiveness (Jer 31:20) a new and eternal covenant has been formed. As Israel returns joyfully to the land (Jer 31:4-5), the new promise will be successful because God will put into the hearts of the people the power to respond. "I will place my law within them, and write it upon their hearts" (Jer 31:33).[5]

As powerful and prominent as the stories of the Exile are, so, too, do images of Israel as a landed people also abound. While Israel dwelt in the land of Egypt, the people had security, at least as far as bodily survival needs were concerned. Yet Israel chose the desert and freedom over land and slavery. The experience of the Exodus (i.e., the choice between slavery and freedom) was not a one-time decision. Because life in the wilderness was also intolerable, the decision had to be made over and over. Could it be that the fleshpots of Egypt, slavery included, were the promise of land made to Abraham? The Israelites were plagued with doubts.

The moment Israel arrives at the Jordan and is about to cross into the "promised land" after forty years of wandering in the wilderness is a moment of radical transformation. From Genesis 12:1 ("Go forth from the land of your kinsfolk . . . to a land that I will show you") to Joshua 21:43 ("And so the Lord gave Israel all the land he had sworn to their fathers he would give them"), Israel had learned to accept, rely on, and celebrate the God who sustains them. Their survival, life itself, particularly in the precarious wilderness, is God's gift. To cross this border means that everything changes. From wilderness to fertile land, from slave to heir, from problem to promise, Israel's needs will now be satisfied in a way that is not chancy or vulnerable but guaranteed. Israel's future is secure.

The land is a gift; Israel did not earn it, does not own it. The land binds them in new ways to Yahweh. "The Jordan is entry not into safe space but into a context of covenant."[6] In the desert Moses stressed obedience to Yahweh. Later, during the period of the monarchy, David stressed land management over Torah. Holding these two pieces of the tradition together (obedience/Torah and land management; see Gen 2:15-17) is a central challenge for Israel.[7]

The land is also a temptation, because land is a source of power. To remember that Yahweh is the source of the gift is to acknowledge that Israel is not in control. Moses gave this warning:

---

[5] Though most translations use the plural word "hearts" in this passage, the Hebrew word used here is the singular "heart." It is the community that responds together to God's promise.

[6] Brueggemann, *The Land* (Philadelphia: Fortress Press, 1977) 53.

[7] Ibid., 52.

> Otherwise, you might say to yourselves, "It is my own power and the strength of my own hand that has obtained for me this wealth." . . . But if you forget the LORD, your God, and follow other gods, serving and worshiping them, I forewarn you this day that you will perish utterly (Deut 8:17, 19).

Torah is the law of Sinai, but Brueggemann argues that "Torah exists so that Israel will not forget whose land it is and how it was given to us."[8] Despite the words quoted above from Joshua 21:43, Israel did not have complete acquisition of the land. Many tribes living in Canaan became a challenge to the newcomers. The Book of Judges is a series of stories of folk heroes and heroines who delivered the people from this "oppression" (i.e., wrested another bit of land for the Israelites). These stories are presented in the framework of a theology of land. In this framework the people sin, and God allows them to fall into the hands of their enemies (i.e., struggle over land possession); when the people cry out, God sends a savior to deliver them. Each story ends with a note about how long the land was at peace as a result of the deliverance achieved by the savior-judge.[9]

This theology only becomes clear to Israel from the perspective of exile. As each new piece of land was acquired, the people began to long for a system of governance that acknowledged their achievements and provided security. Hence the monarchy. Israel's choice of a model like other nations ("appoint a king over us, as other nations have": 1 Sam 8:5) is in opposition to Moses' warning before the border crossing. The prevalent notion of kingship included control of the land as a possession. This kind of possession of the land is in direct opposition to the conditions surrounding Yahweh's land promise. Samuel describes what kingship for Israel will be like:

> Samuel delivered the message of the LORD in full to those who were asking him for a king. He told them: "The rights of the king who will rule you will be as follows: He will take your sons and assign them to his chariots and horses, and they will run before his chariot. He will also appoint from among them his commanders of groups of a thousand and of a hundred soldiers. He will set them to do his plowing and his harvesting, and to make his implements

---

[8] Ibid., 61.

[9] Leslie Hoppe, O.F.M., proposes that the survival of the indigenous people of Canaan is God's judgment upon an unfaithful Israel (Judg 2:20-21); God permits the survival of the Canaanites as a test to determine if Israel will obey God's commands (Judg 2:22). *Joshua, Judges* (Wilmington, Del.: Michael Glazier, 1982) 105.

of war and the equipment of his chariots. He will use your daughters as ointment-makers, as cooks, and as bakers. He will take the best of your fields, vineyards, and olive groves, and give them to his officials. He will tithe your crops and your vineyards, and give the revenue to his eunuchs and his slaves. He will take your male and female servants, as well as your best oxen and your asses, and use them to do his work. He will tithe your flocks and you yourselves will become his slaves. When this takes place, you will complain against the king whom you have chosen, but on that day the LORD will not answer you (1 Sam 8:10-18).

Despite this clear warning, the people persisted. Seduced by the same desire for autonomy that struck Adam and Eve, Israel wanted a king. This land, once a place for human joy and freedom, gradually becomes a land exploited and oppressed under the monarchy. This shift from the notion of land as gift to land to be grasped will eventually cause Israel to lose its hold.

The prophets knew that Israel was headed for exile long before the Israelites did. Comfortable and secure in the land, the Israelites could neither hear nor understand what the prophets were trying to tell them. Of all the prophets, Jeremiah speaks most often and most eloquently about the land. He tells the whole story of Israel as the story of the land. Jeremiah knew that the land must be held with gratitude and a sense of newness. If the grasping of land the way royal Israel held it continued, the land would be lost. In the call of Jeremiah (Jer 1:4-10) it is made clear that Yahweh's initiative will prevail over the reluctant young man, over kings, and over possession of the land. Part of the call of Jeremiah is the announcement with certainty that the land will be lost: "From the north . . . evil will boil over upon all who dwell in the land. . . . Each king shall come and set up his throne at the gateways of Jerusalem" (Jer 1:14-15). Jeremiah carries in his person a deep anguish for Israel. He pleads for repentance: "Be circumcised, remove the foreskins of your hearts" (Jer 4:4), but repentance is not forthcoming.

Israel is numb, apathetic. The covenant has been forgotten. They are not accountable to Yahweh and are not caring for the poor. They practice idolatry and live immoral lives. Remember the warning given in Deuteronomy: When you have plenty to eat, nice houses, flocks and herds, silver and gold, if you forget the Lord your God you shall surely perish (see Deut 8:11-20). Yahweh's judgment is catastrophe: "The besiegers are coming from the distant land. . . . Your conduct, your misdeeds, have done this to you. . . . You struck them, but they did not cringe. . . . one and all, they had broken the yoke, torn off the harness" (Jer 4:16, 18; 5:3, 5). Jeremiah embodies the great public crisis that is about to happen between Yahweh and Jeremiah's contemporaries.[10] "Yet I, like a trusting lamb led to slaughter, had not realized that they were hatching plots against me" (Jer 11:19). Yahweh responds, lamenting the necessary ravaging of Judah: "The LORD has a sword which consumes the land, from end to end: no peace for all mankind" (Jer 12:12).

Land and covenant, inheritance and fidelity, go together. Forgetting the covenant meant forgetting the conditions of the land promise. Dialogue with Yahweh was required, but Israel had lost its ability to hear. In mind and heart the community, under the leadership of the monarchy, had become self-seeking. They wanted autonomy and thought they had achieved it. Because of a lack of justice, Israel lost its inheritance, the land. Jeremiah grieves for the land: "Is this man Coniah a vessel despised, to be broken up, / an instrument that no one wants? / Why are he and his descendants cast out? / Why thrown into a land they know not? / O land, land, land, / hear the word of the LORD" (Jer 22:28-29).

Over and over in the narratives of the Old Testament, Israel's relationship with Yahweh is shown to be inseparable from Israel's relationship to the land. Israel moves from security in the fleshpots of Egypt to emptiness in the wilderness, from joy in the gift of a homeland to control of the land, and then to exile and weeping in Babylon. It would seem that exile is the end of God's chosen people. Without land, there is no history. But what happens in Babylon is the most amazing part of this story.[11] Yahweh has willed this loss, so to cling to the land is wrong. Those who remained in Jerusalem are considered "bad figs" (Jer 24:2) because of their indifference to God's wrath. God has departed from the place that refuses to take God seriously. God is with the "excellent figs" outside the land and promises to "look after them for their good, and bring them back to this land" (Jer 24:6).

Exile, loss, discontinuity, radical as it seems, is the way to new life in new land. To embrace the place of exile is the way to reconciliation.[12] Through Jeremiah, Yahweh tells those in exile to build houses, take wives, have children, and seek the welfare of the city, to pray to the LORD on behalf of this place of exile, because in its welfare they will find their welfare (see Jer 29:5-7). The very place that would seem to be the end of Israel is the place where they will find a new beginning, if, of course, they remain in total reliance on God.

---

[10] Brueggemann, *The Land*, 110.

[11] Brueggemann calls this the "central scandal of the Bible." *The Land*, 122.

[12] This paradox is a familiar one from the New Testament. In Luke's Gospel we read: "For whoever wishes to save his life will lose it, but whoever loses his life for my sake will save it" (Luke 9:24).

When the Jews were led to captivity in Babylon in 586 B.C.E., they found Jewish communities already well established there since the previous exile ten years before. Nearly fifty years later, when the Jews were allowed to return to Jerusalem, only a fraction did so. The majority stayed in Babylon.[13] For the Jews in the Diaspora,[14] the Holy City, Jerusalem, is their mother city, their homeland, yet where they were born and choose to remain is their fatherland. This double attachment—to Jerusalem as homeland and the place of their birth as homeland—still exists today among Jews living outside the state of Israel.

So when Ezra and Nehemiah chronicle Israel's return to Jerusalem, they are speaking of a portion of the Jewish community. Significant reforms take place in Jerusalem. The people want to show they have learned their lesson. During this period the nature of "Jewishness" becomes institutionalized around Torah and Temple. The covenant and land promise are focused on Jerusalem. It is a time of law and order, purification and reconstruction. The particular offenses to be avoided are mixed marriage, not honoring the sabbath, and economic manipulation of citizens by their leaders. Judaism's sense of itself as religiously distinct was honed in hostile Babylon and brought to fulfillment in Jerusalem. Those who stayed in the cities of the Diaspora continued the study of Torah and religious practices. Rabbis developed the doctrine of "God's Presence in Exile,"[15] making life in exile more amenable. The connection to the "land" of Israel became an emotional, religious connection, not a reality.

In Jerusalem a new threat to observance of the tenets of Jewish faith was the subtle influence of Hellenism. The Jews considered themselves distinct and separate, while Hellenism had a new vision of universal humanity. This influence was not a hostile takeover that Israel could fight against. Many aspects of Hellenistic ideology came via a seductive attraction to intellectual enlightenment. Hellenism aimed to make a Greek city out of the Jewish temple state. Though much can be said about the effects of Hellenization on Judaism, the only aspect to be considered here is the change in understanding of land ownership. In

---

[13] Nathan Ausubel, in *The Book of Jewish Knowledge* (New York: Crown Publishers, 1964, 126–127), cites the Hellenistic-Jewish philosopher Philo (ca. 25 B.C.E.–45 C.E.), as the source for these population figures: three million Jews in Judea, more than a million in Egypt, and twice that number in Babylonia-Persia, Cyrenaica, and elsewhere.

[14] "Diaspora" refers collectively to all the geographic places where Jews lived outside Israel.

[15] "*Galut*," in *The Encyclopedia of Judaism*, ed. Geoffrey Wegoder (New York: Macmillan Publishing Co., 1989) 275–277.

Hellenistic politics the land was the personal possession of the king. Thus, old patterns of inheritance were being restored during the Hellenistic period. While the Jews relied on traditional claims to the land, others found ways to take it from them.

There were three distinct responses to this invasion of new politics. All of them help set the stage for land theology in the New Testament. One response was the Maccabean movement; the peasantry fought for land held in covenant. The Maccabeans believed that unless Israel resisted Hellenism by every means, Israel and Judaism would lose their distinct identity. The Maccabees identified Judaism with a devotion to Zion (Jerusalem) and the Temple. A second response was a resurgence of a reflective wisdom tradition. Those who espoused this response chose to ignore this new way of thinking and to be faithful to Yahweh and the old values. They relied on the promise that God's will would prevail. A third response, adopted by some Jews, was a change in vision to accommodate reality. The faithful Jews who found that their economic and political situation did not match the claims and promises of their religious heritage took on an apocalyptic view. They yearned for a new age; their land is land in hope, not land in possession. And so these Jews waited for a better future.

The covenantal land promise made to Abraham, codified into law by Moses, and central to Jewish religious tradition seemed at a point of readiness for transition. At least three circumstances contributed to this readiness. More than half of the Jewish population was scattered around the world, living in foreign lands, faithful but unwilling to return to Israel. The Jews in Jerusalem were divided among themselves on significant religious issues, thus even further weakening any possibility of national unity. The growing menace of the Roman Empire and the politics of land ownership under the influence of Hellenistic standards imposed a governmental system that contradicted traditional Jewish claims to the land. The land had given the Jews both their identity and their history. A new era was about to begin. The stage was set. The destruction of Jerusalem in 70 C.E. by the Romans brought about a new exile, which lasted almost nineteen hundred years. The struggle, often violent, that continues today in Israel/Palestine has, at least for some, the remnant threads of the land promise made to Abraham.

Land Theology in the New Testament

The significance of the land takes a different turn in the New Testament. Various Jewish responses to Hellenism's invading intellectual and political tentacles would set the stage for land theology in the first century. The Jewish people were once again under the thumb of a foreign power, the Roman Empire. The Jews had developed a distinct society for themselves based on the covenant and Temple worship. For them, there was no separation of religion and politics.

The Maccabean revolt (166–160 B.C.E.) aimed to preserve this Jewish society. The Maccabees had been suppressed, but in the first century C.E. there were those who still looked for a military leader who could restore Jewish leadership. Many Jews set their hope on a messiah who would overcome this domination and establish Jerusalem once and for all as the worship center of Judaism. Meanwhile, the world-weary Jew took on an apocalyptic view of Yahweh's land promise. If not now, then in a new age the covenant promises would be fulfilled. One's duty now was to be as faithful as possible to the Law.

Thus, there was division among the Jews. Some began to accept the underlying philosophy of Hellenism and were looked upon by "faithful" Jews as traitors. Jesus of Nazareth entered the world amid this intellectual, political, and religious disarray as an itinerant preacher. The message and presence of Jesus, as told to us by Paul and the Gospel writers, changed the "covenant" from a covenantal land promise centered on Israel to a new covenant in Jesus Christ for the whole world. Christianity's roots are in Judaism, and all that has been said about the inseparable relationship between the land, the people, and God is a significant part of Christian history. The land itself has been made holy by the presence of Abraham and Sarah, Isaac and Rebecca, Jacob and Rachel, Moses and Miriam, Joshua, Judith, Esther, Deborah, Isaiah, Jeremiah, Huldah, and all those, real or mythical, who are our spiritual kin and have provided the story that is the basis of our faith. Anyone who desires to know that history intimately will gain in understanding by knowing the land intimately.

That said, it must be admitted that the lens through which we looked at our biblical history, the lens of land as the basis for theology, becomes almost opaque in the New Testament. We know very little about the place of the land in the minds and hearts of the early Christians. Expectations about the land of Israel were a preoccupation for Jerusalem Jews at the turn of the millennium. Even though Judaism was less centered in the land after the Exile, the Jewish Christians must have come to terms with this age-long yearning of their own history. It is likely that the word "land" took on a symbolic meaning: that of a future hope referring to a spiritual possession beyond history.[16] The documents we have are silent on this transition from land as concrete evidence of the covenant to land as symbol. Instead, Christians have

---

[16] A. J. Tambasco, "Four Biblical Questions," *Chicago Studies* 32 (1993) 160.

generally thought about Judaism in intellectual and theological terms. The encounter between the realia of Judaism[17] and primitive Christianity is a rather recent pursuit of scholarship.

A look at the significance of geography and place in the New Testament will show that a major transition has taken place. The covenant relationship between God and creation which we first hear about in Genesis and which continues throughout the Old Testament has been replaced by a new covenant and a new creation. The gift is no longer the land; the gift is the Son, Jesus. Consequently, the meaningfulness of "the land" recedes as a foundational aspect of faith. The best that can be done to illustrate a land theology of any kind is a review of the literary use of geography and specific places in the New Testament. This review will begin with the writings of Paul and continue through each of the Gospels in chronological order.

Paul was a Jew, a Pharisee, and a Roman citizen. He was born in Tarsus, the Hellenistic capital of the province of Cilicia. He was well educated and would have been familiar with the doctrine of the land in Jewish tradition.[18] In his writings Paul is quite clear that in Christ a new age has dawned. He explained to his listeners that the Torah was a temporary intervention, a custodian between the promise to Abraham and the coming of Christ (Gal 3:23-26). Now the Torah was no longer necessary. Salvation was no longer attached to the Jewish people centered in the land. Now that Christ, the Messiah, has come, salvation is centered in him (Gal 3:19f.). The land that was promised to Abraham has been transformed into and fulfilled by the new life "in Christ." The land, like Torah, particular and provisional, had become irrelevant.[19] In the Letter to the Romans, Paul explains that all of creation, including the land, shares in the divine life, possessed by and subject to the Spirit.[20]

> I consider that the sufferings of this present time are as nothing compared with the glory to be revealed for us. For creation awaits

[17] W. D. Davies, *The Gospel and the Land* (Berkeley: University of California Press, 1974) 161. The Jewish festivals, pilgrimages and liturgy have more significance in some New Testament documents than has generally been perceived.

[18] Paul himself tells us, "I progressed in Judaism beyond many of my contemporaries among my race, since I was even more a zealot for my ancestral traditions" (Gal 1:14).

[19] Davies, *The Gospel and the Land,* 179.

[20] See Charles D. Myers, Jr., "Epistle to the Romans," *Anchor Bible Dictionary,* 5:816–830, and John Pilch, "Romans," *The Collegeville Bible Commentary,* ed. Dianne Bergant, C.S.A., and Robert J. Karris, O.F.M. (Collegeville, Minn.: The Liturgical Press, 1989) 1080–1099.

with eager expectation the revelation of the children of God; for the creation was made subject to futility, not of its own accord but because of the one who subjected it, in hope that creation itself would be set free from its slavery to corruption and share in the glorious freedom of the children of God (Rom 8:18-21).

In Mark's Gospel, Nazareth is mentioned as a bit of biographical information about Jesus (1:9). Later, in Mark 6:1-6, Jesus is teaching in his hometown. His own people are offended by his words, and Jesus cannot do any miracles there because of their unbelief. Nazareth is a place of rejection. Galilee is the place where Jesus attracts crowds. One has to break through the roof to get to him (2:4). Jesus must preach from a boat because of the crowd (4:1). Mark uses words such as mountain (3:13; 6:46; 9:2); the water's edge (1:16; 2:13; 3:7; 4:1); boat (4:1, 36, 37; 5:2, 18, 21; 6:32-54; 8:10); the other side (4:35; 5:21); at home or the house (2:1; 3:20; 7:17, 24; 9:28); a deserted place (1:35, 45; 6:31, 32); and synagogue (1:21-39; 3:1; 6:2) but few actual place names.[21] Galilee would not have been called a holy land by Mark, even though it is the place of new beginning where Peter and the disciples will see the risen Lord (16:7). Jerusalem is a semantic opposite of Galilee.[22] Jerusalem is the capital, the center. Here, instead of crowds and followers, Jesus draws opponents. Jerusalem is the city of ultimate rejection where Jesus must go to die (Mark 10:33).

In Matthew's Gospel we read, "Blessed are the meek for they will inherit the land" (Matt 5:5), but this is not the land of Palestine promised to Abraham in Genesis 17:8 or the land promised to the poor in Psalm 37:11 but the kingdom of heaven.[23] Matthew follows Mark in his contrast between Galilee and Jerusalem. Jerusalem is continually shown to be the city that kills the Messiah. This is in contradiction to Judaism's assumption that Jerusalem will inevitably be the messianic center.[24] "From that time on, Jesus began to show his disciples that he must go to Jerusalem and suffer greatly from the elders, the chief priests, and the scribes, and be killed and on the third day be raised" (Matt 16:21).

In the parable of the wedding feast, Jesus speaks of an angry king who "sent his troops, destroyed those murderers, and burned their city" (Matt 22:7) because they refused the invitation to the feast. Jeru-

---

[21] Davies, *The Gospel and the Land*, 240.

[22] Augustine Stock, *The Message and Method of Mark* (Wilmington, Del.: Michael Glazier, 1989) 59–60.

[23] John P. Meier, *Matthew* (Wilmington, Del.: Michael Glazier, 1980) 40.

[24] Davies, *The Gospel and the Land*, 241.

salem and its Temple were destroyed by the Romans in 70 C.E. Matthew's Gospel was written within short memory of that disastrous event. Its readers would understand the reference here to mean those publicly religious people in Jerusalem who rejected Jesus.

Matthew places the cry of Jesus over Jerusalem at the close of the anti-Pharisaic discourse ending with "your house [temple] will be abandoned, desolate" (Matt 23:38). In the passion narrative, the Jewish leaders are hostile toward Jesus (26:4). Jerusalem is not the holy city but the guilty city. It is in Matthew's Gospel that cities in Galilee are cursed. Chorazin and Capernaum are rebuked by Jesus because so many of his great works had been done there but they did not repent (Matt 11:20-24). In fact, the people of Galilee may have been interested in and attracted to Jesus for a time but did not become true disciples. There is nothing significant about Galilee for Matthew, with the exception that the final scene in the Gospel takes place there. From a "mountain" in Galilee the disciples are directed to "go . . . and make disciples of all nations" (Matt 28:19). In contrast to the Jewish claim to rootedness in a distinct, particular place, the new covenant will break through all geographic boundaries. The gospel is for all nations.

Luke's Gospel is written for Gentile Hellenistic Christians. One does not find here the references to Judaism's land doctrine that are evident in Matthew. Luke uses geography as a literary device, not as a guide to the land. The movement in this Gospel is toward Jerusalem, the center of Luke's story. Jesus' final journey begins with the solemn announcement: "When the days for his being taken up were fulfilled, he resolutely determined to journey to Jerusalem" (Luke 9:51). For Luke, Jerusalem is the geographic center of Christian beginnings.[25] Writing of the fall of Jerusalem for Christian Gentiles, Luke connects the destruction of the Temple with the beginning of the era of the Gentile mission (Luke 21:20-24).[26]

In the Acts of the Apostles, the movement is away from Jerusalem, again beginning with a solemn announcement: "But you will receive power when the holy Spirit comes upon you, and you will be my witnesses in Jerusalem, throughout Judea and Samaria, and to the ends of the earth" (Acts 1:8). The focus now is on the universality of salvation. From Jerusalem the ministry of the disciples moves outward to Judea and Samaria, then to Asia Minor and Europe.[27]

The Gospel of John shows an ingenious concern for "holy space." Several examples illustrate the author's genius in transforming a holy

---

[25] Ibid., 260.

[26] Jerome Kodell, O.S.B., "Luke," *The Collegeville Bible Commentary*, 974.

[27] Wesley I. Toews, "Book of Luke-Acts," *Anchor Bible Dictionary*, 4:403–420.

place in the Jewish tradition to a place made holy by the action of Jesus. When Jesus speaks to Nathaniel, he says, "Amen, amen, I say to you, you will see the sky opened and the angels of God ascending and descending on the Son of Man" (John 1:51). The unifying of heaven and earth that Jacob saw in a vision (Gen 28:12), causing him to create a sanctuary at Bethel, Nathaniel sees before him in the person of Jesus. The cleansing of the Temple occurs in John 2:13ff. Jesus' purification of the Temple is symbolic of the destruction of the Temple, which has already occurred at the time the Gospel is written. The Temple's function will be replaced by the risen body of Jesus.

The meeting with the Samaritan woman in John 4:1-15 is another example of a holy place replaced. Jacob's well at Shechem provided water, but Jesus tells the woman at this place that he will provide living water. In the second part of this passage (John 4:16-25), Jesus tells the woman that worship will not be on Mount Gerizim, the mountain holy to the Samaritans, or in Jerusalem, but "true worshipers will worship the Father in Spirit and truth." Jesus is the source of the Spirit in whom alone worship "in spirit and truth" is possible.

The five porticoes of the pool at Bethesda (John 5:1-9) might be symbolic of the Torah. The waters here were not able to heal the paralyzed man, but Jesus does it with a word. The blind man was healed by Jesus and told to wash in the pool of Siloam (John 9:1ff.). These are the same waters referred to in Isaiah 8:6 as Shiloah,[28] a place of healing waters. In its tradition Israel looked forward to "life," which for them meant being in the Promised Land flowing with milk and honey, centered in Jerusalem. In the Fourth Gospel, "life" also plays a significant role; "life" is always centered in Jesus, who has become the "space" where life is to be found.[29]

The Book of Revelation has the final word on sacred space in the New Testament. "Like bookends enclosing the entire corpus of biblical reflection, the opening chapters of the Book of Genesis and the closing chapters of the Book of Revelation alert the reader to God's irrevocable alliance, for better or for worse, with the created world."[30] John foresees "a new heaven and a new earth" (Rev 21:1), which will replace the old creation, just as the author of Third Isaiah prophesied: "Lo, I am about to create new heavens and a new earth" (Isa 65:17). John also sees "the holy city, a new Jerusalem, coming down out of heaven from God" (Rev 21:2). This description is reminiscent of Jacob's ladder, a

[28] Davies, *The Gospel and the Land*, 314.

[29] Ibid., 331.

[30] Barbara E. Bowe, R.S.C.J., "A New Heaven and a New Earth," *The Bible Today* 33 (1995) 33.

"break in space" linking heaven and earth. The city is holy because God dwells there with us. The dimensions given to this city in Revelation are such that it could be the whole earth.[31]

In the New Testament, words such as "land" and places such as "the temple" and "Jerusalem" become concepts that are nongeographic, often used in a spiritual, transcendent sense as symbols of eternal life beyond space and time. The message of the new geography is that salvation, friendship with God, is not limited to a particular people or a particular place but is universal, including all creation, all people.

Yet, history and geography need to be remembered. Jesus did become incarnate in a particular place. Where this happened becomes significant. Jesus did die and was raised in Jerusalem, thus lending glory to this place and every place where he was. To have a felt sense of the land, to feel its heat or dryness, to see its hills and deserts is to better understand the visual world of Jesus. On the other hand, the risen Lord is not confined to any particular place. To do justice to these two concepts—the Jesus of time and space and the Christ of faith—we must understand the theology of land that formed the Old Testament, the only Scriptures Jesus knew. We hold the land reverently, careful not to grasp it too tightly, for the New Testament story extends "to the ends of the earth" (Acts 1:8), and thus in a real way makes all land holy.

[31] Ibid., 37.

The roadway down the Mount of Olives is steep and narrow as it winds past the Russian Church of Mary Magdalene on its way to the Church of All Nations at the Garden of Gethsemane. In the far left is the Golden Dome on the Temple Mount.

1. The Mount of Olives

Scripture Readings

Cycle A	1st Sunday of Advent	Matt 24:37-44
	32nd Sunday of Ordinary Time	Matt 25:1-13
	33rd Sunday of Ordinary Time	Matt 25:14-30
	34th Sunday of Ordinary Time	Matt 25:31-46
Cycle B	1st Sunday of Advent	Mark 13:33-37
	33rd Sunday of Ordinary Time	Mark 13:24-32

About the Site

In each of these Gospel passages Jesus is speaking from the same geographic location, the Mount of Olives. The Mount of Olives is part of a ridge of hills that overlooks Jerusalem from the east. The ridge is two and a half miles long and has three summits. The highest summit, Mount Scopus, is at the north end, 2,690 feet above sea level. It is from Mount Scopus that one coming from the north would have the first view of Jerusalem and the Temple.

The Mount of Olives is the second summit, 2,660 feet in height. It is directly across from the city and the Temple area. The village of Bethany is located on a ridge adjacent to the Mount of Olives to the southeast. Directly east of the Mount of Olives the Judean Wilderness drops thirty-nine hundred feet over a distance of fifteen miles to the Dead Sea.

Farther south on the ridge, lower than the other two peaks and opposite the southern wall of the Temple area, is the third summit, called the Mount of Evil Counsel. Here Solomon's foreign wives worshiped false gods (2 Kgs 23:13).

Between the Mount of Olives and Jerusalem is the Kidron Valley. Water was brought into the city by aqueduct from the Gihon Spring in this valley to the pools of Siloam. In the eighth century B.C.E., Hezekiah built a tunnel (2 Kgs 20:20) to channel the water into the walled city and deny it to the attacking Assyrians. Three godly kings of Judah (Asa, Hezekiah, and Josiah) burned idols in this valley. Tombs built during the second Temple period are still visible in the valley. It is a twenty to twenty-five-minute steep walk from the Temple area through the valley to the gardens on the Mount of Olives.

Reflection

Mountains are holy places, close to God. In the New Testament, Matthew has six major mountain scenes.[1] One of these is the apocalyptic discourse in chapters 24 and 25, which takes place on the Mount of Olives. Mark parallels this location in chapter 13, where Jesus predicts the destruction of the Temple. Perched on the Mount of Olives looking west, one can see in a great panorama the whole history of Jerusalem. The remnants of David's City and the splendor of the Temple first built by Solomon bring to mind the glory days of the monarchy and the United Kingdom, dating approximately to the tenth century B.C.E.

Jerusalem was a fortified city built on a hill. The city was situated along a trade route and had a plentiful water supply. These characteristics made it possible for Jerusalem to be a lasting city and a good choice for the capital of a kingdom. David brought the ark of the covenant to Jerusalem, making this city the center of worship for the Israelites. Solomon enhanced this center for worship by building a Temple for Yahweh, yet he also supported pagan temples built outside the city. Succeeding kings worked to purify the Jewish religion by eliminating other forms of worship. Descendants of David ruled here until the time of the Exile in the sixth century B.C.E.

The destruction of Jerusalem and the Temple and the consequent exile to Babylon in 586 B.C.E. challenged many theological assumptions held by the Israelites. The land was part of Yahweh's covenant promise. Losing the land meant that this relationship with God (and the nation that went with it) was over, gone, lost, ended. The covenant was broken. The Israelites were no longer Yahweh's chosen people.

During the Exile a new perspective and a new hope developed. Yahweh was a faithful God to whom the Israelites had been unfaithful. Being expelled from their land was a just punishment, but it was only temporary. The Exile would be a time of acknowledging their unfaithfulness, a time of purification and rededication of themselves to Yahweh. Jerusalem became a symbol during the Exile as well as a concrete place to which they longed to return. Jerusalem, on Mount Zion, replaced Sinai as the central mountain of Israel's religion.

---

[1] The temptation, 4:8; the Sermon on the Mount, 5:1; the healing of many people, 15:29; the transfiguration, 17:1-9; the apocalyptic discourse, 24–25; the final commissioning, 28:16-20. Benedict Viviano, "Mountain," *Collegeville Pastoral Dictionary of Biblical Theology*, ed. Carroll Stuhlmueller (Collegeville, Minn.: The Liturgical Press, 1995) 650–654.

In days to come,
The mountain of the LORD's house
    shall be established as the highest mountain
    and raised above the hills.
All nations shall stream toward it (Isa 2:2).

In the six Gospel passages that have Jesus speaking from the geographic location of the Mount of Olives, he is looking at nine hundred years of Israel's history laid out before him. He says to his disciples (and to us) that once again *it is over.*[2] Gazing directly at the splendid, grandiose Temple built by Solomon, destroyed, rebuilt and most recently enhanced by Herod the Great in Jesus' lifetime, he speaks of a new kingdom that is coming. What we have known is to be wiped out in the way Noah's world was destroyed by the flood, in the way the Jewish world was ended at the time of the Exile. Jesus presents a clear vision of the future: expect to suffer; in the end God will establish the longed-for kingdom.

The liturgical cycle of readings reminds us at the beginning of Advent that we are about to celebrate the most radical event in the history of the cosmos, the Incarnation. Now is the opportunity to start over. So stay awake, be watchful.

---

[2] Both the Gospel of Mark and the Gospel of Matthew were written at the time of, or shortly after, the destruction of the Temple by the Romans in 70 C.E.

The Wilderness of Judah is a desolate, empty, lonely land, the haunt of nomads. Its length is approximately thirty-five miles from north to south, and its width fifteen miles east to west (from barely a half mile east of Jerusalem to the Jordan River). The road in the foreground descends into the Wadi Qelt, today a national park.

2. The Wilderness of Judah

Scripture Readings

Cycle A	2nd Sunday of Advent	Matt 3:1-12
	1st Sunday of Lent	Matt 4:1-11
Cycle B	2nd Sunday of Advent	Mark 1:1-18
	3rd Sunday of Advent	John 1:6-8, 19-28
	1st Sunday of Lent	Mark 1:12-15
Cycle C	2nd Sunday of Advent	Luke 3:1-6
	3rd Sunday of Advent	Luke 3:10-18
	1st Sunday of Lent	Luke 4:1-13

About the Site

The Israelite tribe of Judah descended from the man Judah, the fourth son of Jacob and Leah (Gen 29:35). After Joshua's death, this tribe was the first to occupy its allotted territory in the southern hill country of Canaan, a mountainous region around Jerusalem.

Geography played a major role in the history of Judah. For example, Judah was separated from the rest of the Hebrew tribes that lived to the north by rough and wild land, with deep east-west valleys. The distance from Hebron (south of Jerusalem) east to the mountains of Moab is approximately thirty-six miles as the crow flies but requires a descent from three thousand feet above sea level to thirteen hundred feet below sea level, the lowest point on earth, and up again to three thousand feet. This challenging land form was not the sole cause of the division between the kingdoms of Israel and Judah, to be sure, but in effect it kept them apart, just as railroad tracks or a major highway divides some cities into separate entities.

Geography also determined the administrative classification of the cities of Judah into four major regions: the Negev (south), the Shephelah (lowlands), the hill country, and the wilderness (Josh 15:21, 33, 48, 61).[1] The Wilderness of Judah is an area approximately thirty-five miles from north to south (from Jericho to Qumran along the northwest end of the Dead Sea) and fifteen miles east to west (from barely a half mile east of Jerusalem to the Jordan River). The area is a desolate,

---

[1] Yohanan Aharoni and Michael Ave-Yonah, *The Macmillan Bible Atlas* (New York: Macmillan, 1968) 14.

empty, lonely land, the haunt of nomads, uncultivated and therefore not permanently settled. The type of rock found here is called marl—loose, crumbling earth made of sand, salt, or clay. This soft chalky rock erodes easily. Wind and rushing runoff from higher lands to the west create deep east-west canyons, making north-south travel impossible.[2] The average annual rainfall is from zero to four inches; the temperature ranges from 16 to 36 degrees centigrade with thirty percent humidity.

It was in this wilderness that Saul pursued David (1 Sam 24), John the Baptist lived, preached, and baptized, Jesus was tempted, and hundreds, perhaps thousands, of men and women gave birth to desert monasticism in the second and third centuries C.E.

It may be that John chose this area because of his association with the community at Qumran, where he may have been raised.[3] A central tenet of the Qumran community is embodied in Second Isaiah: prepare for what lies ahead. They chose the austerity of the wilderness as a way of separating themselves from city life and Temple worship. Their purpose was to study and *do* the Law of God in order to "prepare the way" for God's new coming. The introduction of John as precursor by all four Gospel writers includes the words of Isaiah 40:3: "A voice cries out: In the desert prepare the way of the LORD" (Matt 3:3; Mark 1:3; Luke 3:4; John 1:23). Scripture testifies to John's austere lifestyle (Mark 1:6), another feature he shares with the Qumran community.

John imitates and resembles Elijah (2 Kgs 1:8); he speaks the words of Isaiah (40:3). Yet John differs from the Qumran way of life in at least one significant way: he preaches. He attracts great crowds. "People of the whole Judean countryside and all the inhabitants of Jerusalem were going out to him . . . (Mark 1:5)." John provides a ritual of baptism, symbolizing a person's willingness to change and God's willingness to forgive sins. It is not enough that a select group, the Essenes, prepare themselves for the coming of the Messiah; John calls for a change of heart from the other two major sects within religious Judaism, the Pharisees and the Sadducees[4] (Matt 3:7) and suggests that salvation is not hereditary, hinting that Gentiles, too, may be saved (Matt 3:9).

---

[2] Paul Wayne Ferris, Jr., "Wilderness of Judah," *Anchor Bible Dictionary,* ed. David Freedman (New York: Doubleday, 1992) 3:1037.

[3] Joseph Grassi, "John the Baptist," *The Collegeville Pastoral Dictionary of Biblical Theology,* ed. Carroll Stuhlmueller, C.P. (Collegeville, Minn.: The Liturgical Press, 1996) 492.

[4] Benedict Viviano, O.P., "The Gospel According to Matthew," *New Jerome Biblical Commentary,* ed. Raymond Brown, S.S., Joseph Fitzmyer, S.J., Roland Murphy, O.Carm. (Englewood Cliffs, N.J.: Prentice Hall, 1990) 637.

Reflection

The desert is exquisitely beautiful, although hot, dry, desolate, harsh, unforgiving. The desert is a place where people always live in a survival mode, looking for water and food, a place where one is utterly alone and very vulnerable. One's fears emerge: fear of heights, of darkness, of illness, of being lost, of not being in control. The desert, the wilderness, is a place each of us has experienced sometime, perhaps many times, in our life. The wilderness is the perfect place to prepare for a new coming of God into our world, not because God lives in the wilderness but because the wilderness strips one of self-sustaining supports, leaving one open to God's initiative.

The image and symbol of desert are used at critical turning points in the journey of biblical spirituality. The Israelites were called out of Egypt to wander and survive through nearly two generations in the wilderness. When Cyrus, king of Persia, urged the Jews to return to Jerusalem from their exile in Babylon, they had to cross the Wilderness of Judah to get there. Now John the Baptist "prepares the way" for the Messiah in the same Wilderness of Judah by preaching repentance and baptizing with water.

The desert is a place of great contrasts. The sun and heat scorch the landscape during the daylight hours, while clear, starry skies reign over cold nights. At first glance, it seems that nothing could bloom in the desert, yet some of the most exquisite vegetation can be found there, with root systems and stems adapted for survival. The surprise flower or bush is all the more delicate, precious, and beautiful because of its surroundings. In the midst of harsh climate and hardship, there is hope for life. A sudden rain can make the desert area bloom with grass in a matter of hours. Just below the apparently barren surface abundant life is waiting to be freed.

Like his desert surroundings, the image of John is fierce and stern. He is a prophet whose demands for change are simple but radical. His challenge is to empty oneself; his baptism with water is a ritual of cleansing away the past to prepare for something new.

A theme throughout these gospel readings is that of a third Exodus.[5] The miracles of the Sinai desert experience will recur (see Isa 35:1; 41:19; 51:3). The temptations will recur also, but Jesus will overcome them. The total destruction of Jerusalem, the loss of land, the pain of brokenness that marks the time of exile presents the opportunity for a paradigm shift, a new relationship, a renewed covenant with God.

---

[5] The first Exodus was the escape from Egypt to the Promised Land; the second was the return from Babylon to Jerusalem.

Desert wilderness is a place of transformation, of letting go, of empty-ing, in order to be filled and changed by the Spirit. This time of Advent (or Lent) is an invitation to each of us to enter into the wilderness so that God's initiative may once again emerge from the desert through us.

Lower Galilee is dotted with Arab and Jewish villages. Nazareth Illit in the background is a suburb of the city of Nazareth.

3. Towns, Villages, and Synagogues

Scripture Readings

About the Sites

In Jesus' day, the Galilean countryside was peppered with 204 villages, according to the first-century Jewish historian Josephus.[1] The major cities of Tiberias and Sepphoris are not mentioned by the Gospel writers, and Jesus may have purposely avoided them, though he does go to Jerusalem and Caesarea Philippi in northern Galilee (Matt 16:13; Mark 8:27-29).

The name Sepphoris comes from the word *zippor*, meaning "bird," so named because it sits like a nesting bird atop a hill above the Bet Netofah valley. When Herod Antipas inherited Galilee after his father's death, the formerly fortified city was in ruins. Following his father's penchant for great construction projects, Herod Antipas began rebuilding the city in 3 B.C.E. Scholars speculate that the building of this Roman city may have encouraged Joseph to move his family to Nazareth, a Jewish village nearby. During the building campaign at Sepphoris, he would have found work for many years. The inhabitants

---

[1] William Whiston, *The Works of Josephus* (Peabody, Mass.: Hendrickson, 1995) 15.

of this newly built city were wealthy landowners and members of the priestly elite.

The composition of Tiberias was quite different. On the shores of the Sea of Galilee, Tiberias was populated by anyone Herod Antipas could entice to settle there, since the city had been built on an ancient cemetery. Herod, following his father's example at Caesarea Maritima, founded this new city and named it in honor of his patron, the emperor Tiberius. At its completion in 20 C.E., Tiberias usurped Sepphoris's title as the capital of Galilee.

Herod Antipas wasn't the only son of Herod the Great to engage in construction. While Herod Antipas was rebuilding Sepphoris, his brother Philip constructed Caesarea Philippi, which became the capital of his territory north of the Sea of Galilee. During the same building campaign, Philip "advanced the village Bethsaida [where Peter and Andrew were from], situated at the lake of Gennesaret [Galilee], unto the dignity of a city, both by the number of inhabitants it contained, and its other grandeur" (*Antiquities*, 18:28).[2]

Although a few major cities enjoyed a good economy because of construction, the rural area of Galilee suffered from overpopulation and double taxation by the Romans and the Jewish Temple. The majority (90 percent) were peasants, eking out a living through farming. Village life was communal, most villagers claiming kinship with one another. The land farmed by peasants either belonged to an absentee landlord (part of the 10 percent of elite in first-century Palestine) or was ancestral property, passed on through generations. As successive regimes claimed authority over Palestine, those ancestral properties were whittled away until many former landowners became landless tenants farming what had once been their own property.

Though dotted by small villages, Galilee was not isolated. Trade routes connected rural villages with coastal cities. The ease of access and the industry around the lake created a more cosmopolitan character. Jewish and non-Jewish populations seemed to interact readily, evidenced by various archaeological findings and the Gospel writers' acknowledgment that Jesus frequented the Decapolis, a non-Jewish area.

Reflection

Today many of the tiny hamlets between Nazareth and Capernaum still cling to rocky escarpments or nestle close to the lake's edge. At night one can more easily see the numerous settlements, as house lights dot the black hillsides. Most of these villages are Arab settlements now.

---

[2] Ibid., 478.

The towns closer to Tiberias are Jewish. The distance from Nazareth to Capernaum is about thirty miles, downhill, through fertile valleys and lush hills.

The towns, villages, and synagogues of Galilee became the backdrop of much of Jesus' teaching and healing. But we know very little about him prior to his public ministry. According to Luke (3:23), he began when he was about thirty years old. He accompanied his parents on a trip to Jerusalem as an infant (Luke 2:22), returning there every subsequent Passover with his family (Luke 2:41). Matthew sends Jesus and his family to Egypt after his birth and then moves the family to Nazareth (Matt 2:13). Most of his life was spent in and around Nazareth, the hillside Jewish village a few miles from the Roman city of Sepphoris. After his baptism by John, probably on his return from pilgrimage in Jerusalem, Jesus began a ministry of healing and preaching, marked by travels through Galilee.

In the Sunday gospels associated with towns, villages, and synagogues, particularly chapter 9 of Matthew's Gospel, Jesus demonstrates extraordinary healings: the woman with the flow of blood, the official's daughter, two blind men, a mute demoniac (9:8-34). Surrounded by need, he is "moved with pity" (Matt 9:36; the original Greek is much more forceful: *splagchnizomai*, referring to one's innards; Jesus has a gut response to the pain and suffering he sees). Recognizing the immensity of the needs, he summons the Twelve and sends them out. In Mark's Gospel, it is after Jesus' rejection in his own hometown of Nazareth that he calls and sends out the Twelve. In both Gospels, the apostles are given instructions for the journey. Their task is a continuation of Jesus' own work: preaching and healing. Only in Luke's Gospel does this setting become part of the larger journey to Jerusalem, and the focus is not one of healing but of parabolic discourse.

In the time of Jesus, a large number of homeless would have wandered these valleys, hoping for day labor. Jesus' sending of the Twelve in pairs was probably more a response to the dangers of travel than a concern for companionship. The land of Lower Galilee, like much of the rest of first-century Palestine, was embroiled in tension. Each town evidenced its own caste system, with a few elite occupying the central positions of power and the non-elite surrounding this nucleus. The vast majority lived outside the walls of the town. They were the beggars, prostitutes, persons in undesirable occupations, and landless day laborers. They could enter the town by day but were locked out at night.[3] The lack of land, employment, and food increased sickness and

[3] Bruce Malina and Richard Rohrbaugh, *Social-Science Commentary on the Synoptic Gospels* (Minneapolis: Fortress, 1992) 85.

disease. People eagerly gathered to hear a preacher proclaim a better life, a possible release from the sin that was their lot.

When Jesus curses the towns of Chorazin, Bethsaida, and Capernaum (Matt 11:20-24) for failing to repent, we can surmise that it is the walled elite to whom he refers and not the peasantry. Nazareth rejects his message, and he can do no great work there apart from a few healings (Mark 6:1-6). Who would stand to benefit from Jesus' proclamation of good news? Who would stand to lose?

That question is even more unsettling when asked today. Our North American "towns and villages" have reversed the walls. Now we often wall in our poor and scurry to the safety of the suburbs. When a healer proclaims a different manifesto, one challenging the status quo, he or she is quickly attacked, dismissed, and chased out of town. Perhaps that was Luke's vision in using these settings for his parabolic discourse. He was writing for a more urban and cosmopolitan community. For them, parables could cut through their cynicism and lay bare the truth, cauterizing the wound of division, greed, and status. The "towns and villages and synagogues" and churches today are not terribly different. Perhaps what has changed is the side of the wall on which we find ourselves.

Hennessy, Anne, C.S.J. *The Galilee of Jesus.* Rome: Editrice Pontificia Universita Gregoriana, 1994.

Hoppe, Leslie J. *Joshua, Judges.* Wilmington, Del.: Michael Glazier, 1982.

Jabusch, Willard. *Walk Where Jesus Walked.* Notre Dame, Ind.: Ave Maria, 1986.

Johnson, Luke Timothy. *The Gospel of Luke.* Sacra Pagina Series. Collegeville, Minn.: The Liturgical Press, 1991.

Johnson, Sherman E. *Jesus and His Towns.* Good News Studies. Wilmington, Del.: Michael Glazier, 1989.

Lane, Belden C. *Landscapes of the Sacred.* New York: Paulist Press, 1988.

Laymon, Charles M., ed. *The Interpreter's One-Volume Commentary on the Bible.* Nashville: Abingdon, 1971.

Malina, Bruce. *The New Testament World: Insights from Cultural Anthropology.* Louisville, Ky.: Westminster/John Knox, 1993.

Malina, Bruce, and Richard Rohrbaugh. *Social-Science Commentary on the Synoptic Gospels.* Minneapolis: Fortress, 1992.

Matthews, Victor. *Manners and Customs in the Bible.* Peabody, Mass.: Hendrickson, 1988.

Mays, James Luther, ed. *Harper's Bible Commentary.* New York: Harper & Row, 1988.

McRay, John. *Archaeology and the New Testament.* Grand Rapids, Mich.: Baker, 1991.

Meier, John P. *Matthew. New Testament Message.* Wilmington, Del.: Michael Glazier, 1980.

Meinardus, Otto. *The Holy Family in Egypt.* Cairo: American University Press, 1963.

Miller, Max. *Introducing the Holy Land.* Macon, Ga.: Mercer University Press, 1982.

Murphy-O'Connor, Jerome, O.P. *The Holy Land.* New York: Oxford University Press, 1992.

_____. "Why Jesus Went Back to Galilee." *Bible Review* 12 (February 1996) 21.

Newsom, Carol, and Sharon Ringe, eds. *The Women's Bible Commentary.* Louisville, Ky.: Westminster/John Knox, 1992.

Neyrey, Jerome H., ed. *The Social World of Luke-Acts.* Peabody, Mass.: Hendrickson, 1991.

Ousterhout, Robert, ed. *The Blessings of Pilgrimage.* Chicago: University of Illinois Press, 1990.

Bibliography

Achtemeier, Paul J., ed. *Harper's Bible Dictionary*. San Francisco: Harper & Row, 1985.

Aharoni, Yohanan, and Michael Ave-Yonah. *The Macmillan Bible Atlas*. New York: Macmillan, 1968.

Baly, Dennis. *Basic Biblical Geography*. Philadelphia: Fortress, 1987.

Barrett, C. K. *The Gospel According to St. John: An Introduction with Commentary and Notes on the Greek Text*. London: SPCK, 1978.

Beane, Wendell, and William Doty, eds. *Myths, Rites, Symbols: A Mircea Eliade Reader*. New York: Harper & Row, 1975.

Beitzel, Barry J. "The Via Maris in Literary and Cartographic Sources." *Biblical Archaeologist* 54 (June 1991) 64–75.

Brown, Peter. *The Cult of the Saints: Its Rise and Function in Latin Christianity*. Chicago: University of Chicago Press, 1981.

Brown, Raymond E., S.S. *The Birth of the Messiah*. New York: Doubleday, 1993.

Brown, Raymond, S.S., Joseph Fitzmyer, S.J., Roland Murphy, O.Carm., eds. *The New Jerome Biblical Commentary*. Englewood Cliffs, N.J.: Prentice Hall, 1990.

Brownrigg, Ronald. *Come, See the Place: The Ideal Companion for All Travellers to the Holy Land*. London: Hodder and Stoughton, 1985.

Brueggemann, Walter. *The Land*. Philadelphia: Fortress, 1977.

Charlesworth, James. *The Old Testament Pseudepigrapha*. New York: Doubleday, 1983.

Dillard, Annie. *Teaching a Stone to Talk*. New York: Harper & Row, 1982.

Eliade, Mircea, ed. *The Encyclopedia of Religion*. New York: Macmillan, 1987.

_____. *The Sacred and the Profane*. New York: Harper & Row, 1959.

Finegan, Jack. *The Archaeology of the New Testament: The Life of Jesus and the Beginning of the Early Church*. Princeton, N.J.: Princeton University Press, 1992.

Freedman, David Noel, ed. *The Anchor Bible Dictionary*. Vols. 1–6. New York: Doubleday, 1992.

Freeman-Grenville, G.S.P. *The Holy Land: A Pilgrim's Guide to Israel, Jordan and the Sinai*. New York: Continuum, 1996.

Harpur, James. *The Atlas of Sacred Places*. New York: Henry Holt, 1994.

A statue of the Annunciation greets pilgrims before they enter the basilica.

4. Nazareth

Scripture Readings

Cycle B	4th Sunday of Advent	Luke 1:26-38
	14th Sunday of Ordinary Time	Mark 6:1-6
Cycle C	3rd Sunday of Ordinary Time	Luke 1:1-4; 4:14-21
	4th Sunday of Ordinary Time	Luke 4:21-30

About the Site

There is no mention of Nazareth in the Old Testament, the Talmud, the Midrash, or Josephus. This is not an indication that Nazareth did not exist, only that it was apparently insignificant (John 1:46). Excavations show that the site of the modern town of Nazareth was a settled place from about the third century.[1] After the First Jewish Revolt (168 B.C.E.) the priests, who were categorized in twenty-four divisions, fled northward from the Temple in Jerusalem. One of these priestly families settled in Nazareth. A Hebrew inscription found at Caesarea Maritima in 1962 lists priests who lived in Nazareth at the time Jesus would have lived there. In addition, the kokhim tombs[2] found there reflect a style of tomb used by Jews up to 70 C.E. These archaeological finds provide evidence that Nazareth was a Jewish settlement in the Roman period.[3] Christian sources record a third-century martyr named Conan, who claimed to be from Nazareth and a member of Jesus' family.

Nazareth is in Lower Galilee, north of the Jezreel Valley. The village is built on the sides of a hill in a valley that opens only to the south. The elevation is approximately thirteen hundred feet. From the hilltop looking west one sees Mount Carmel, to the east Mount Tabor, to the north Mount Hermon, and to the south the Plain of Esdraelon (Jezreel). The Sea of Galilee is fifteen miles east, the Mediterranean Sea twenty miles west. The altitude, its protected position, and twenty-five inches of rainfall annually make for a moderate climate favorable to vegetation.

[1] Jack Finegan, *The Archeology of the New Testament.* (Princeton, N.J.: Princeton University Press, 1992) 46.

[2] "Kokhim" refers to a tomb chamber for up to nine bodies, sometimes sealed with a rolling stone.

[3] Sherman E. Johnson, *Jesus and His Towns*, Good News Studies (Wilmington, Del.: Michael Glazier, 1989) 26.

Tombs found to the north, south, and west, which would have been outside the village, give some idea of the limits of the settlement. Nazareth would have been about sixty acres in size, sustaining a population between one hundred and four hundred, a small village devoted wholly to agriculture.[4] Silos for grain, cisterns for water and oil, presses for raisins and olives, and many millstones testify to the work of the villagers. The village was secluded and not on any main highway, though Japha, one and a half miles southwest, was used by Josephus as headquarters for military operations during the Jewish war, and Sepphoris, three miles north, was an important city.

A small village would have welcomed the services of Joseph, a carpenter, and his son (Mark 6:3). The larger cities within a reasonable walking distance would have provided more than adequate business. Joseph's handiwork probably included yokes, plows, chests, and furniture, and he would have been responsible for transporting and installing ceiling beams in village homes.[5]

Every Jewish village had a synagogue, which served as a secondary place of worship while the Temple in Jerusalem still existed. The synagogue also served as a meeting place and a center for the study of Scripture.

Reflection

Nazareth is a place of surprises. The earliest mention of Nazareth in the New Testament (i.e., in the chronological life of Jesus) is in the beginning of the Gospel of Luke (1:26). The scene described here is a perfect example of an event that marks a place as sacred. Nazareth, in the first century, was a tiny rural village where one would think life went on quietly in its humdrum way, with nothing significant to share with the outside world. Yet God chose this simple place to break into our world again in a way that had not happened since Moses encountered God on Mount Sinai. A young woman here was not frightened or put off by the appearance of an angel. Mary carried on quite a remarkable dialogue with this celestial being. She trusted that the messenger and the message were from God.

Many books have been written about Mary's *fiat*. Her wholehearted response to God's plan, her faith in the presence and power of God, became the foundation for a theme of Luke's Gospel: God's promise of salvation is fulfilled in Jesus. Mary's faith-response is a

---

[4] James Strange, "Nazareth," *Anchor Bible Dictionary,* ed. David Freedman (New York: Doubleday, 1992) 4:1050.

[5] Victor Matthews, *Manners and Customs in the Bible* (Peabody, Mass.: Hendrickson, 1988) 251.

In a second-story window, a young boy looks out over the bustling city of Nazareth.

total contrast to the faith-response of the townspeople many years later when Jesus preached in the synagogue.

There were more surprises to come out of Nazareth. It was in the setting of this small village that we come face to face with the stark reality of the Incarnation. Jesus was a real person with a history, a family, a place of origin, neighbors, people who knew him, but he discovered that it is difficult, perhaps impossible, to be recognized as an expert on anything at home.

Luke places Jesus in the synagogue at Nazareth at the beginning of his ministry in Galilee. In the Gospel of Luke, Jesus comes home "in the power of the Spirit" (Luke 4:14) immediately after his baptism and the challenge of the devil in the desert. Mark brings Jesus to Nazareth toward the end of his Galilean ministry, after he has worked many healing miracles and has established a following. In either case, Jesus is a stumbling block for the people of Nazareth. They cannot see beyond the face of the man they knew as a boy. His words are not prophetic to them; they are pretentious.

The Jesus we meet here (Luke 4:14-30) is a teacher, a good public speaker, especially when addressing a group about God. We don't know how long it has been since he's been home or if he has ever spoken in this synagogue as an adult before. What he says astonishes the people. His news is another surprise coming out of Nazareth, namely, that God's plan of salvation is fulfilled in ministry to the poor and unfortunate. The reading from Isaiah that Jesus chooses from the scroll[6] is a reminder of the jubilee year, that is, the observance every fifty years when fields lay fallow, debts were canceled, and slaves were set free. The image presented is one of restoration, new beginning, and a conviction that the structures of social and economic life must reflect God's reign.

In his comments after the reading, Jesus gives clear indication that God's promised salvation will extend beyond the Jews. The people are surprised by this interpretation and do not like it. Elsewhere this message is well received. At home the people "take offense at him" (Mark 6:3), are "filled with fury" (Luke 4:28), and try to kill him. We read these words matter-of-factly today, but the incident is really quite startling. How often does a congregation try to kill a preacher whose words are offensive?

One of the purposes for which Gospel writers tell this story is to prepare us for Jesus' ultimate rejection and death; there will be persecution and opposition from within the synagogue. But in addition to this foreshadowing of events to come, there is much to contemplate in Jesus' experience and his response in this particular setting. It takes strength, integrity, and the courage of one's convictions to continue speaking aloud in the face of opposition, especially from people you know and love. God's power in Jesus is not diminished when he is in Nazareth, but because it is not received, it is not integrated into the faith of the people—it is impotent. The message of Isaiah 61 that the structures of social and economic life must reflect equality, justice, and mercy for all is not only a message for Jesus' historical "today" but is for *our* today.

The surprises coming out of Nazareth—the angel and young woman conversing, the announcement of the Messiah, the news that God's plan of salvation extends beyond the Jews, the condition that this plan of God requires justice for the poor—are all surprises that we must discover "at home" in our own village, in our own quiet, seemingly insignificant life and faith.

---

[6] This reading actually would not be found on a Torah scroll. What is quoted in the Gospel story is an artistic weaving together of Isaiah 61:1-2 and Isaiah 58:6.

Among the hectic streets of the city are quiet alleys where men play dominos and drink Turkish coffee.

This road leads down from the Church of the Visitation. In the center of the Jewish village of Ein Karem is the Church of John the Baptist.

5. Ein Karem

Scripture Reading

Cycle C   4th Sunday of Advent   Luke 1:39-45

About the Site

Ein Karem is a village in the hill country at a point about five miles equidistant from Jerusalem and Bethlehem. The name means "spring of the vineyard." The rolling hills are covered with olive groves, orchards, and vineyards; brilliantly colored flowers bloom everywhere, making the area picturesque. The place is believed to be where Zechariah and Elizabeth had their home and where John the Baptist was born. The Gospel writer Luke says that Mary "traveled to the hill country in haste to a town of Judah" (Luke 1:39). John's birth, and especially the events surrounding his naming, were talked about "throughout the hill country of Judea"(Luke 1:65). The Greek word for "hill country" is the same as the Latin word used by Pliny in his *Natural History,* completed in 77 C.E., to refer to the region around Jerusalem.

The writings of the pilgrim Theodosius (530) mention the distance from Jerusalem west to the place where Elizabeth lived as five miles. The Gregorian festival calendar, which lists the places where the Jerusalem Church celebrated festivals of the Church year before 638, mentions Ein Karem by name.[1]

Archaeological excavations show that Ein Karem was continuously occupied from 2000 B.C.E. Coins have been found confirming occupancy during the Herodian period. The significant remains, however, are from the Byzantine period (324–638). These remains indicate that Ein Karem, as the birthplace of John, was revered by the early Church as a pilgrimage or festival site.[2]

In Ein Karem, houses are shaded by cypress and pine trees. The soil is dark and well cultivated. It is difficult to grow crops such as corn and barley there because of the steep hillsides and stony fields. Farmers over the centuries have used the stones to terrace the hillsides for

---

[1] Jack Finegan, *The Archaeology of the New Testament* (Princeton, N.J.: Princeton University Press, 1992) 3–5.

[2] Jerome Murphy-O'Connor, O.P., *The Holy Land* (Oxford: Oxford University Press, 1992) 155.

use as vineyards and orchards. Stone towers dot the hillsides. For two thousand years these towers have been used by villagers to take refuge from the summer heat and to look after the orchards.[3]

Today Ein Karem is a village of artists and delightful outdoor cafes. Two twentieth-century churches in Ein Karem commemorate the events inspired by the Gospel narratives. The Church of St. John on the northern hill honors the birth of John the Baptist. The Church of the Visitation on the southern hill commemorates both the visit of Mary and Elizabeth and the hiding of the infant John. Here paintings of Old Testament figures in the upper church—Sarah, Rachel, Miriam, Deborah, Jael, Judith, Esther, and Anna—give testimony to the continued powerful influence of women throughout covenant history. These women are the foremothers of Mary and Elizabeth. They are present here as midwives of the transition from the old to the new covenant.

Reflection

Accounts of events in Ein Karem come from tradition. The *Protoevangelium of James,* written about 150, includes the story of Elizabeth's pregnancy and her decision to await the birth of her child in the seclusion of the country home she and Zechariah had in Ein Karem. Further in James's account we learn that when Herod set out to slaughter boys under the age of two, Zechariah would not reveal the whereabouts of his infant son and so was killed in the Temple. Elizabeth fled, again to their country home, where God miraculously saved mother and child by hiding them in a rock.

These traditions and the paths made by the feet of the pilgrims who have gone before us, more than archaeological proof, lead us to this oasis of charming beauty a few miles from Jerusalem. The detailed stories of Mary's visit with Elizabeth, John's birth, and his escape from the murderous Herod give color and faith-value to the historical finds of archaeology. The land and ambience of Ein Karem provide the setting for the biblical events we believe took place here. The land itself helps create the image of the event and in so doing leads us to insights for our own life and faith.

Elizabeth, despite a long married life, is childless. Now, when it seems that she is past her childbearing years, she becomes pregnant. She chooses to go to a more secluded place, perhaps for the solitude and peaceful atmosphere, to await the birth of her firstborn. In her place of seclusion Elizabeth receives a visitor, Mary, a young relative

---

[3] Maria Teresa Petrozzi, *Ain Karem: The Holy Places of Palestine* (Jerusalem: Franciscan Printing Press, 1971) 29.

who is also pregnant. The two women, full of the joy of new life growing within them, meet in a place surrounded by lavish growth and the
sweet scent of fruit trees bearing figs, apples, pears, pomegranates,
mulberries, and walnuts. How appropriate that these two women, ripe
with the fruit of their own bodies, are surrounded by precious, abundant, vibrant new life! It is the mature vines that give the best grapes
and the new fruit fresh from the trees that have the best taste. Both
women can find in the surroundings of Ein Karem models of new life
in nature to give them hope and courage that the seeds planted within
them will come to fruition as successfully as everything they see
around them.

Mary and Elizabeth are certainly among the most significant women
in the New Testament. The relationship between them is also significant, as evidenced by what happened when they came together. Mary
set out "in haste" to visit Elizabeth. Perhaps Mary was worried about
her cousin's health, but more likely she could not wait to share the joy
of their mutual good fortune. At the sound of Mary's voice, the infant
in Elizabeth's womb leapt for joy. What love must have been expressed
in that greeting!

The intimacy, intensity, depth, and beauty of a profound friendship
are revealed in this brief description of how these women felt when
they met each other in Ein Karem. Elizabeth knew what was in Mary's
heart and affirmed the recent action of God in Mary's life before Mary
spoke the words (Luke 1:43). Each knew the faith-life of the other. They
had likely shared their faith with one another before, and, like the
physical surroundings of Ein Karem, faith shared grows and is fruitful.

The steeple in the foreground, seen from the rooftop of the Giacaman Brothers' woodshop, marks the spot of Jesus' birth.

6. Bethlehem and Shepherds' Field

Scripture Readings

Cycle A	4th Sunday of Advent	Matt 1:18-24
Cycles A, B, C	Christmas at Midnight	Luke 2:1-14
Cycles A, B, C	Epiphany	Matt 2:1-12

About the Site

Two Bethlehems are mentioned in the Bible. Bethlehem in Zebulun was seven miles northwest of Nazareth and is mentioned in the Book of Joshua (19:15). This Bethlehem may have been the home of Ibzan, one of the minor judges (Judg 12:8-10).[1] Bethlehem of Judah, also known as Ephrathah in Genesis 35:19, is five and a half miles south of Jerusalem. In Hebrew, Bethlehem can mean "house of bread," probably because of the wheat fields surrounding it.

This latter Bethlehem gained notoriety for its famous son David. Anointed by the prophet Samuel here, David became the first king of Israel, uniting the northern and southern tribes. Because of this, the future king was expected to come from here:

> But you, Bethlehem-Ephrathah,
> > too small to be among the clans of Judah,
> From you shall come forth for me
> > one who is to be ruler in Israel,
> Whose origin is from of old,
> > from ancient times (Micah 5:1).

The same passage is quoted by Matthew to make explicit connection between Jesus' birth and the messianic hope.

Since the second century, the cave commemorated as the place of Jesus' birth was considered sacred. The first Church of the Nativity, built over the site by Queen Helena, mother of Emperor Constantine, was dedicated in May 339. Today the cave appears as a narrow room, a few steps below the altar. A silver star embedded in marble marks the site of the birth. The area has been so built up that aside from the

---

[1] Paul J. Achtemeier, ed., *Harper's Bible Dictionary* (San Francisco: Harper & Row, 1985) 107.

The Church of the Nativity looks more like a fortress than a holy site.

depth, one can hardly imagine it as it must have once appeared. Visiting the nearby caves of St. Jerome provides the visitor a better sense of its original design. St. Jerome translated the Hebrew Bible into Latin while living in the caves from 386 until his death in 420.

The Church of the Nativity was rebuilt and enlarged in 529 by Emperor Justinian and survived various invaders, largely due to the fact that the Muslims had been permitted to hold some of their devotions in its space. The great center door is walled up, so that one must bend at the waist to enter. This was done as a protective measure in the thirteenth century to prevent looters from entering on horseback. From the outside, the Church of the Nativity looks more like a fortress than a holy place, witnessing to its tumultuous history.

Reflection

Today, from the roof of the Giacaman family's workshop, Joseph Giacaman points to the metal-framed star attached to a nearby church roof. The star stands above the spot commemorated since the second century as the site of Jesus' birth. To be Christian in Bethlehem is no easy task, he comments. He and his family are some of the few Palestinian Christians still residing in the Holy Land. Economic restraints, political unrest, and harassment from Israelis and Palestinian Muslims have forced many indigenous Christians to leave their land. But this bright July afternoon, Joseph beams with pride. He and his family have stayed, operate a successful shop specializing in olive wood sculptures, and humbly boast that their shop is only a short distance away from the site of the manger.

Few sites in the Holy Land are considered "authentic," that is, actual sites where the event they commemorate occurred. The Church of the Nativity in Bethlehem, the Holy Sepulcher in Jerusalem, and the House of Peter in Capernaum are perhaps the three sites with the most supporting evidence. So when the Giacaman family gather with the throngs in Manger Square on Christmas Eve, they celebrate not only the birth of Jesus but the birth of their faith, which reaches from ancient Bethlehem "to the ends of the earth" (Acts 1:8).

"Here [in Bethlehem] he was wrapped in swaddling clothes; here he was seen by the shepherds; here he was pointed out by the star; here he was adored by the wise men," writes St. Jerome (Ep. 46:10).[2] Jerome weaves together in a few phrases major differences between the Infancy Narratives of Matthew and Luke. In Matthew, magi (from which we get our term "magician"), probably Persian astronomers, arrive in Jerusalem, following a star that indicated the birth of a king. In Luke, a learned elite are not the first to acknowledge Jesus' birth. Quite the opposite. Consistent with Lukan theology, it is the poor and outcast who hear the angels. Shepherds were considered the riffraff of first-century Palestinian society. They slept with the animals in the field, leaving their wives alone, and grazed their animals on others' pastures, taking what was not theirs.[3] Thus the birth of Jesus is recognized by two distinct groups, according to the Gospel writers' developing theology. What is consistent is that both locate the events of Jesus' birth in Bethlehem.

If, as Luke says, Joseph is returning to his ancestral land for the census, he would have family in the town. When he mentions "inn," Luke may be referring to the guest room attached to some peasant houses. That the guest room is occupied may mean that a family member of higher rank has returned for the census as well.[4]

Homes of this period were often built in front of a cave cut into the soft limestone. The addition served as the family area, while the animals were housed in the back. The manger, or feedbox, separated the

---

[2] Cited by Robert Wilken, *The Land Called Holy: Palestine in Christian History and Thought* (New Haven, Conn.: Yale University Press, 1992) 120.

[3] Bruce Malina and Richard Rohrbaugh, *Social-Science Commentary on the Synoptic Gospels* (Minneapolis: Fortress, 1992) 296.

[4] Ibid., 297.

Thistles bloom in a valley near Shepherds' Field.

two areas. The warmth of the animals in the back radiated throughout the residence, providing a natural heating system, particularly during the chill of winter. These caves still serve a similar purpose today. Bedouin shepherds build corrals in front of the caves, providing their sheep some protection from the weather.

Today the Crèche Orphanage, attached to the Holy Family Hospital run by the Daughters of Charity in Bethlehem, provides care for abandoned or orphaned children. Pilgrims often prefer to see the Holy Land as "places frozen in a biblical time frame,"[5] but the truth is that Bethlehem is no serene hamlet of Christmas song fame. As in any city, children are born to alcoholic parents and single mothers unable to care for them. Families are poor and cannot afford to feed another child. The Crèche becomes home for all the children, whether Palestinian Christian or Muslim, whose stars are not noticed by the rich and the wise.

While Bethlehem is a sprawling Arab city today, shepherds still upset traffic with their flocks. Leading out of the city, down the steep hillside, roads follow a circuitous route, probably the paved paths trod by flocks long ago. As the valley widens east of the city, one passes

[5] Wilken, *The Land Called Holy*, xiii.

Shepherds' Field, a tourist stop on the pilgrim's tour. But one need only travel a few miles in either direction to see the true descendants of those first-century shepherds, still herding in the traditional way. Young boys chase the delinquent sheep and goats, while older men sit in groups off at a distance.

As night comes, the herds are gathered near a Bedouin camp of black tents. The sun drops suddenly and the night sky is bright with stars. On Christmas one star does shine directly over Bethlehem; it is the star that Joseph Giacaman pointed out—the metal one with light bulbs on the roof over the site of Jesus' birth. But no longer do wise people from the East or West note its light or hasten toward it. Angels are hoarse from too many "Alleluias" left unheard. "Peace on earth, good will toward all" is a faint echo, and it is sometimes only the stalwart who hear—people like the Giacaman family, Joseph and his sister Angela and his brother Issa. People like the Daughters of Charity, Sister Paschal and Sister Mary Catherine. Perhaps there is no multitude of the heavenly hosts proclaiming the glory of the Christian God here in the Holy Land. But . . .

> Without the presence of living Christian communities, the witness of the Holy Land can only be equivocal. The martyrs and teachers, the monks and bishops, the faithful who lived in Bethlehem and Beit Jala and Nazareth and Jerusalem would no longer be signs of a living faith, but forgotten names from a distant past. Bethlehem would become a shrine, and Christian Jerusalem a city of ancient renown. Only people, not stones and earth and marble, can bear an authentic witness.[6]

[6] Ibid., 254.

A woman and her daughter sell rag dolls near Luxor.

7. The Flight into Egypt

Scripture Reading

Cycle A   Feast of the Holy Family   Matt 2:13-15, 19-23

About the Site

In biblical tradition, Egypt was a land of refuge for those fleeing trouble in Palestine. The brothers of Joseph sought relief from famine in Egypt (Gen 42:1-38). Jeroboam fled to Egypt when King Solomon sought to kill him (1 Kgs 11:40). The prophet Uriah escaped the sword of King Johoiakim in the same way (Jer 26:21).[1] And Jeremiah went to Egypt with the remnant of inhabitants of Bethlehem and Jerusalem to avoid slaughter by the Chaldeans during the Babylonian invasion (Jer 42). One possibility for the inclusion of this episode of the flight into Egypt in the early life of the Holy Family is that Matthew was influenced by this "refuge in Egypt" tradition. In addition, this story helps fulfill the prophetic tradition, "Out of Egypt I have called my son" (Hos 11:1).

The distance from Bethlehem to the Nile Delta area of Egypt is two hundred miles across desert. If the Holy Family went to Egypt, they would have joined a caravan rather than attempt this long, difficult, and dangerous journey alone. Most probably they would have traveled the Via Maris, a major caravan route along the Mediterranean coast beginning in Egypt, crossing Palestine, and continuing to Syria. Movement by caravan, even across desert, would average twenty miles a day.[2] The route is still followed today: Ashkelon to Gaza to Rafah to al-Arish to Farama at the edge of the Nile Delta, though the mode of travel has changed considerably.

After the death of Mark Antony and Cleopatra in 31 B.C.E., Egypt became a Roman province. Since Herod's power would not be effective there, Egypt would have been a safe place for those avoiding Herod's ruthlessness. In addition, there were thriving Jewish communities in Egypt, which also made this location a viable possibility for Jews "on the run." Jews had the right of citizenship and were allowed their own magistrates and courts of justice, with free exercise of their own religion. In the first century a million Jews, more wealthy and enlightened than those of Palestine, lived in Egypt.[3]

---

[1] Raymond E. Brown, *The Birth of the Messiah* (New York: Doubleday, 1993) 203.

[2] F. J. Knecht, *Practical Commentary on Holy Scripture* (St. Louis: Herder, 1930) 44.

[3] J. R. Dummellow, *One Volume Bible Commentary* (New York: Macmillan, 1946) 628.

Some scholars suggest that perhaps at most the Holy Family crossed the border into Gaza, a section of land along the Mediterranean coast of Palestine held by Egypt at the time. Others hold that there is no historical evidence at all to support the flight into Egypt by the Holy Family. Meanwhile, the Coptic tradition is full of charming legends about the life of the Holy Family in Egypt. These stories include protection from dragons, reverence by lions and leopards, palm trees that bent down before them to provide both shade and food, wells of water that became a source of healing after being touched by the child Jesus.

One popular tradition takes the family to Babylon, the Roman garrison post over which Cairo was built. Today there is a church in Old Cairo that claims to be the site where the Holy Family lived while in Egypt. This church is near the ancient Jewish synagogue. A well in the floor of the southern sanctuary of the lower church is still used to draw water for the healing of the sick. Many other pilgrimage sites associated with the Holy Family exist throughout Egypt and are reverenced by both Christians and Muslims.[4]

Reflection

> My heart pounds within me;
>> death's terrors fall upon me.
> Fear and trembling overwhelm me;
>> shuddering sweeps over me.
> I say, "If only I had wings like a dove,
>> that I might fly away and find rest.
> Far away I would flee;
>> I would stay in the desert.
> I would soon find a shelter
>> from the raging wind and storm" (Ps 55:5-9).

Thus the psalmist describes vividly the fear of one in need of refuge. Refuge is a place to go when one is in danger or in a situation too difficult to tolerate. Some go to family or friends for refuge. There familiar, welcoming faces, common history, language, customs, and food provide safety and comfort. No words may be needed to explain the visit, the danger that is threatening. Here one is loved and accepted without question. Here, in the midst of security, one can gather the resources needed to return home and face the challenges ahead.

---

[4] Otto Meinardus, *The Holy Family in Egypt* (Cairo: American University Press, 1963). This delightful book contains the complete account of the traditions surrounding the flight of the Holy Family into and through Egypt. The anecdotes have been compiled from both Eastern and Western sources, including both Muslim and Christian traditions.

Awaiting a tourist, a camel rests in front of the Great Pyramids at Giza.

God is a source of refuge. In twenty-six different psalms we hear, "O God, in you I take refuge."[5] The psalmist asks God to hide me in the shadow of your wings (Pss 17:8, 36:8, 61:5). God as a place of refuge is shield (18:31), savior (28:8), rock (31:3; 71:3; 74:22), stronghold (59:17), and fortress (91:2, 144:2). The psalmist prays this prayer not out of helplessness but full of confidence, knowing where consolation and safety are to be found. The psalms provide expression for the whole range of human circumstances. This frequent reference to the encounter with danger or weakness and the need for protection is an indication that these, too, are common human experiences.

[5] Pss 2:11; 5:11; 7:2; 11:1; 14:6; 16:1; 17:7; 18:3; 28:8; 31:2; 34:9; 36:8; 37:39; 46:2; 52:9; 59:17; 61:4; 62:8; 64:11; 71:1; 73:28; 91:2; 94:22; 118:8; 141:8; 142:6.

When seeking refuge, one may have to leave everything behind, not knowing if there will be any opportunity to return. In extreme situations, reported so frequently today in the media, thousands of people must flee their homeland in order to save their lives. There is no time to put the family valuables in storage, to arrange for housing someplace else, to make any plans at all. With a few possessions on their backs and a child by the hand, these refugees flee one danger for another danger, flee certain death for certain insecurity; they are totally vulnerable and dependent on the help and kindness of others.

We do not often think of the Holy Family as refugees. Perhaps it would be good for us to do so. The world's refugees might benefit from a more empathetic and generous attitude toward those who are most vulnerable because they have been forced to flee from life-threatening danger.

Pilgrims rent white gowns and reenact their baptism at the Israeli tourist spot of Yardenit, where the Jordan River exits the southern end of the Sea of Galilee.

8. The Baptism in the Jordan

Scripture Readings

Cycle A	Baptism of the Lord	Matt 3:13-17
	2nd Sunday of Ordinary Time	John 1:29-34
Cycle B	Baptism of the Lord	Mark 1:6-11
	2nd Sunday of Ordinary Time	John 1:35-42
Cycle C	Baptism of the Lord	Luke 3:15-16, 21-22

About the Site

John's Gospel often offers the most accurate geographic locations. While the Synoptics have John come from "the desert" (Mark 1:4) to baptize "in the Jordan River" (Matt 3:6) and "throughout [the] whole region of the Jordan" (Luke 3:3), only John offers a specific location: "Bethany across the Jordan" (John 1:28). This Bethany is distinguished from Bethany on the Mount of Olives, twenty miles west of the Jordan River. Though the oldest texts read "Bethany," some variant readings of "Bethabara" are found. Origen (185–253) asserted that the correct location is "Bethabara," which he located on the west bank of the Jordan. The Madaba Map, a sixth-century mosaic map of the Holy Land found in an ancient church about fifteen miles east of the river, shows Bethabara on the west bank of the Jordan, indicating that John baptized there. By placing Bethabara on the west bank, contrary to the Gospel of John, the map may have relocated the spot for the convenience of pilgrims.

John the Baptist associated himself with Elijah, and the Bordeaux Pilgrim (333) describes the Mount of St. Elijah on the east side of the Jordan. "From there to the Jordan, where the Lord was baptized by John, is five miles. Here there is a place by the river, a little hill on the far bank where Elijah was caught up into heaven."[1] Likely it is then that John's place of baptism was on the east side of the Jordan where pilgrims from the North would have traversed the Jordan on their way to Jerusalem. Today the Monastery of St. John about four and a half miles upstream from the Dead Sea on the west bank of the Jordan commemorates the site of the baptism of Jesus, though probably the actual location was across the river.

[1] John Wilkinson, *Egeria's Travels Newly Translated with Supporting Documents and Notes* (London: SPCK, 1971) 161.

Reflection

The Wadi Qelt plummets more than three thousand feet as it leaves the outskirts of Jerusalem for the Dead Sea valley 1,280 feet below sea level. In the rainy season, this dry riverbed floods, filling cisterns and aqueducts along its fifteen-mile journey to the Jordan River. Along the winding wadi the remains of an old Roman road are visible. For the pilgrims coming from the Decapolis and Galilee, this was the route to Jerusalem. Three of the Gospels mention that the inhabitants of Jerusalem were among those coming to John for baptism (Matt 3:5; Mark 1:5; John 1:19). The journey to the place where John was baptizing would have brought the curious of Jerusalem along this Roman road, through the stark Judean desert down to the Jordan.

Biblical scholar Jerome Murphy-Connor, O.P., suggests that John's baptizing may have taken place during the winter months, when many of Jerusalem's elite stayed in Jericho because of the warm climate.[2] Today the site that commemorates the baptism of Jesus is lush and green where the Jordan bows out and forms several pools, perfect for baptizing the hundreds of pilgrims who visit the site. This is the picture-perfect site, with handrails leading the faithful into the cool, green water after they have rented their white garment at the changing station. But it is some seventy miles north from the area where the baptism of Jesus more likely occurred.

John's ministry may have been a response to his time with the Essenes, a strict, ascetical group that engaged in frequent ritual cleansing. This group may have occupied Qumran, near the caves where the Dead Sea Scrolls were found and only about ten miles from the area where John began his work. The use of water for ritual cleansing in a desert are powerful symbols even today. If John had been a member of a strong religious sect—and there seems to be textual evidence to support this—then it makes sense that his baptism for the forgiveness of sins would have occurred near one of the traditional routes up to Jerusalem.

In addition, after his baptism Jesus "was led by the Spirit into the desert to be tempted by the devil" (Matt 4:1). The Judean Wilderness, rising up from the Dead Sea valley, is a stark landscape of wadis and steep hills. It is likely, then, that after Jesus' profound experience of baptism ("You are my beloved Son; with you I am well pleased"— Mark 1:11), he retreated into this wilderness, pondering what the Spirit of God was moving him to do, reflecting on the power of knowing himself as "beloved" of God. Murphy-O'Connor posits that after Jesus'

---

[2] Jerome Murphy-O'Connor, O.P., "Why Jesus Went Back to Galilee," *Bible Review* 12 (February 1996) 26.

baptism, he followed his relative's lead and joined the baptism ministry (John 3:22). Jesus worked in the area in which John had laid a foundation, while the Baptist took the frontier, the area of Samaria. It was
only after John's arrest that Jesus returned to Galilee "proclaiming the
gospel of God. 'This is the time of fulfillment. The kingdom of God is
at hand. Repent, and believe in the gospel'" (Mark 1:14-15).

It was not the verdant Jordan of Galilee in which Jesus was baptized but the narrowing ribbon of water that pours into the Dead Sea.
He was not surrounded by the mountains of his youth but by the arid
hills of Judea when he heard the voice of God calling him "beloved."
Perhaps here geography becomes an icon for God's action. The desert
places that we avoid may be the very places of baptism in which we
need to be immersed, while the places of comfort we enjoy may be the
Galilee we are called to return to and announce for ourselves, "This is
the time of fulfillment. . . . Repent, and believe in the gospel."

In the distance the Arab village to Tur'an is visible. The road by the village climbs steadily higher past the Horns of Hittin on its way to the Sea of Galilee at Tiberias.

9. Nazareth to Capernaum

Scripture Readings

Cycle A	3rd Sunday of Ordinary Time	Matt 4:12-23
Cycle B	3rd Sunday of Ordinary Time	Mark 1:14-20

About the Site

According to Matthew, Jesus' return to Galilee was in response to the news of John's arrest. While Matthew was not interested in the exact route of Jesus' movements, the sequence of Nazareth then Capernaum, does indicate a specific geography. Traveling through Samaria, the trip from Jerusalem to Galilee took about three days in the first century. By this route Galilean pilgrims returning from Jerusalem would come to Nazareth before Capernaum. If pilgrims took the eastern route across the Jordan, they would have arrived at Capernaum first.

When Jesus traveled up from Judea, he was returning "home" to an area blessed with fertile valleys and plentiful water. Nazareth was then a tiny Jewish village three and a half miles from Sepphoris, the capital of Galilee, home of Herod Antipas until the building of Tiberias in the year 20. Today Nazareth, the largest Arab Christian city in Israel, eclipses the ruins at Sepphoris. Overlooking the east-west Netofah Valley, it is fifteen miles from the Sea of Galilee and about twenty miles from Capernaum. After mounting the plateau near the Horns of Hittin, the Sea of Galilee lies about 696 feet below sea level. The trip from Nazareth to Capernaum thus begins with a long climb up the plain and then a steep decline toward the Sea. The Wadi el-Haman, or Valley of the Pigeons, like most wadis in Jesus' day, provided travelers with a more gentle and steady route than the cresting and plummeting ridges did.

The Romans took advantage of natural roadways like wadis and provided the area with extensive roads, often following older routes. While Matthew's quoting of Isaiah 8:23–9:1 gives us a glimpse into his theological agenda, it also indicates first-century Palestinian trade routes. What would later be known as the "Via Maris," the road of Isaiah or "The Way of the Sea," went southwest from Mesopotamia by way of Damascus, crossed the Jordan, passing by Hazor, then continued southeast to Capernaum and Magdala, where it then went southwest through the Wadi el-Haman. Passing near Nazareth, it followed the Plain of Esdraelon through the pass at Megiddo to the coast of the Mediterranean, where it continued south into Egypt.[1] During the time of the Roman Empire this road not only provided a conduit for trade and transportation but it facilitated communication and allowed for the swift moving of troops. It was also the road Jesus and his followers would have taken between Capernaum and Nazareth.

Reflection

The synoptic Gospels agree that after his baptism and experience in the wilderness, Jesus returned to his native Galilee, though only Matthew and Mark associate this return with John's arrest. If Jesus had continued in the baptizing ministry of his cousin John the Baptist, as John 3:23 insists, then Jesus may have remained in Judah for some time after his initial experience of baptism.

Having taken up the mantle of John, Jesus returns to Galilee with a similar message. While John proclaimed a baptism for the forgiveness of sins, Jesus proclaims "the gospel of God: 'This is the time of fulfillment. The kingdom of God is at hand. Repent, and believe in the gospel'" (Mark 1:15). However, no longer is the ministry one of waiting for repentant sinners to avail themselves of ritual cleansing. Now Jesus sets out. "Come after me, and I will make you fishers of men," he says to his first disciples (Matt 4:19). People went out to John (Matt 3:5), but Jesus' invitation to his disciples is to become "fishers of men." Jesus proposes to go out to the people. "Let us go on to the nearby villages that I may preach there also. For this purpose have I come" (Mark 1:38). The proclamation of Jesus is taken on the road, and the success of his mission is directly related to his ability to travel and reach other listeners.

To assist him in his work, Jesus calls disciples who, given their immediate response to his invitation, seemed to have known of him prior to his call. Yet something more must have encouraged their actions, for "apart from pilgrimage, both geographical mobility and the consequent break with one's social network (family, patrons, friends, neighbors) were considered abnormal behavior and would have been much more traumatic in antiquity than simply leaving behind one's job and tools."[2]

Perhaps it is this desire for itinerancy that sparks Jesus' move to Capernaum, where the Via Maris would allow him easy access to more

[1] Jack Finegan, *The Archaeology of the New Testament* (Princeton, N.J.: Princeton University Press, 1992) 85.

[2] Bruce Malina and Richard Rohrbaugh, *Social-Science Commentary on the Synoptic Gospels* (Minneapolis: Fortress, 1992) 44.

northern points like Caesarea Philippi (Mark 8:27) and the Decapolis (Mark 6:53). In view of Herod Antipas's repressive actions, Jesus may have chosen Capernaum because of its close proximity to the border of the tetrarchy of Herod Philip, into which he and his disciples could easily escape. Capernaum had a toll or tax office (Matt 9:9) and a garrison (Luke 7:2). Its location on the Way of the Sea, or the Via Maris, would provide him with a steady stream of traveling merchants, itinerant workers looking for employment and farmers bringing their produce to market.

Today two hundred sixty kibbutzim dot the landscape of Israel. Whether clinging to the edge of the Mediterranean like Sdot Yam or "making the desert bloom" like Sede Boqer in the Negev, these communities witness to the value of shared life and the possibility of a better life. Jewish immigrants from all over are welcomed and invited to begin anew in Israel. One young couple, both social workers from New York, left their country and kin to join a kibbutz south of Beth Shean near the Jordan Valley. With their three children they have left the comfort of the known and risked a lifestyle that most today would think foolish. What is it that propels the human spirit to let go of the known and risk all? For Jesus? For the first disciples? For the young family of kibbutzniks? Perhaps the answer lies in Jesus' initial invitation, "Come." We first need to be invited.

Reminiscent of the stone jars used by Jesus, these common jars await their usefulness.

10. Cana

Scripture Reading

Cycle C   2nd Sunday of Ordinary Time   John 2:1-12

About the Site

Often sites in the land of Palestine retain their ancient name or a derivative of that name. Such is the case with Cana. Two sites, Khirbet Qana and Kefar Kenna, are both located in the hill country of Galilee, less than six miles apart from each other. Through the ages both have been considered the site where Jesus turned the water into wine. Khirbet Qana, today an unoccupied hill of ruins, is nine miles north of Nazareth. Kefar (meaning "village") Kenna is a small Arab town only four miles from Nazareth. Though literary evidence shows both to have been sites of pilgrimage, archaeological excavations at Kefar Kenna have uncovered ceramics and coins from the Roman and Byzantine periods. Coins dating from Herod the Great (37–4 B.C.E.) show Kefar Kenna to have been an inhabited Jewish village two thousand years ago.

A pilgrim in the sixth century, Anonymous of Piacenza, is the first to speak of a shrine at Cana. He gives the distance from Sepphoris as three Roman miles, the same distance between Sepphoris and Kefar Kenna today. Kefar Kenna has a fresh spring, while Khirbet Qana does not. Various archaeologists hold either Kefar Kenna or Khirbet Qana as the Cana of Jesus' day, though the actual location is uncertain. Today, a church built over the original Byzantine structures and a Franciscan monastery are located in the center of Kefar Kenna. In 1556, while the early Christian church was being used as a mosque, the Greek Orthodox built a church. It was rebuilt in 1886 and is now located on the main highway through town.

Reflection

On the slopes outside Nazareth, Kefar Kenna sits as a sleepy town on a quiet Thursday afternoon. One is through Kenna before realizing, "Hey, that was Cana!" The main road slices through the village and descends into the valley. On either side the town grows up, literally, on the hillside. Secondary roads narrow into driveways and then dead-end into walled yards. An Arab town, Kefar Kenna is peppered with old men in kafiahs sitting around a domino table, and children darting in and out of the open markets, obviously on errands from home. It is easy to picture this town some two thousand years ago.

The Gospel writer John tells us that after meeting John the Baptist and gathering some disciples in Judea, Jesus returns to Galilee. He meets Philip, who is from the hometown of Andrew and Peter. Philip then invites Nathanael, who is from Cana, to "come and see" (John 1:46). Probably coming from Nazareth (his mother's home), Jesus and his disciples go to Cana for a wedding. According to John's Gospel, he performs his first sign, at the urging of his mother.

From here Jesus will go to Capernaum and then to Jerusalem, "since the Passover of the Jews was near" (John 2:13). Interestingly, on his return trip from Jerusalem he will pass through Samaria, encountering the woman at Jacob's Well (John 4) and remaining for two days. He then arrives in Galilee, where he is welcomed (John 4:45). Nazareth lies almost directly north of Shechem, the site of Jacob's Well. Given the proximity of Nazareth to Jacob's Well, we can surmise that he went to Nazareth first. The text then places Jesus back in Cana, where he performs the second sign: healing the royal official's son from a distance. In what seems to be a recurring cycle, Jesus returns to Jerusalem for another feast.

The first sign at Cana gives us a glimpse into Jewish Palestinian life in the first century. A wedding feast is being held, and Jesus, his mother, and his disciples attend. Noticing that the wine is running out, the mother of Jesus, who is never named in John's Gospel, tells her son about this embarrassing prospect. His response surprises modern readers, but it would have been in keeping with the Semitic worldview. He addresses her not as "Mother," as we would today, but as "Woman." Interestingly, the vocative case, used for direct address, is used only a few times in John's Gospel. Jesus addresses his mother (John 2:4 and 19:26), the Samaritan woman at the well (John 4:21), and Mary of Magdala (John 20:15) as "Woman." The only other occurrence of the vocative is when Jesus calls God "Father."[1] Far from making a caustic remark, Jesus is addressing his mother with respect.

In the Mediterranean world of Jesus, respect for one's parents was paramount. The codes of honor and shame fostered a collective sense of identity and worth. The adult males fostered honor through strength, daring, valor, generosity, and wisdom, while adult females promoted positive shame (being concerned about one's honor).[2] In the

---

[1] Adele Reinhartz, "The Gospel of John," *Searching the Scriptures,* ed. Elisabeth Schüssler-Fiorenza (New York: Crossroad, 1994) 569.

[2] Joseph Plevnik, "Honor/Shame," *Biblical Social Values and their Meaning: A Handbook,* ed. John J. Pilch and Bruce J. Malina (Peabody, Mass.: Hendrickson, 1993) 96.

A store in Kefar Kenna sells Cana wedding wine and mineral water.

story of Cana, the mother of Jesus appears to be concerned with pre-
serving the family's honor. Whether Jesus' comment, "How does your
concern affect me?" is a dismissal of his mother's asserting the customs
of honor and shame or if Jesus is simply not ready to "perform," we do
not know. What we do know is that Jesus did respond despite his original hesitancy. The miraculous sign prevents a potential loss of family
honor and, in fact, increases honor for Jesus, and in so doing "revealed
his glory, and his disciples began to believe in him" (John 2:11).

The inhabited village of Kefar Kenna today sits above the Turʾan
Valley (Merj es-Sunbul in Arabic). At the bottom of the hill is a crossroads. Going west will take one to Shefarʾam and eventually Haifa,
while going east takes one up the heights above the Sea of Galilee and
then down into the modern city of Tiberias, about sixteen miles away.
A couple of miles from the crossroads is a pottery factory. In the warm
afternoon light sit hundreds of clay jars and pots, reminiscent of their
famous stone cousins that once upon a time held water turned into
wine. In a land that still today values water as the source of life and
hope and holds wine as sacramental, tiny Cana stands as a reminder
that we are often called to do more than we think we ought. Like the
water jars for purification, we too may be asked to become miraculous
signs of joy, enabling the wedding feast to continue, the host to be
praised, and the glory of God to be revealed so that others may believe.

Through a window in the synagogue, the black basalt walls of the first-century village are visible. In the distance is the Sea of Galilee.

11. Capernaum

Scripture Readings

About the Site

Hugging the shore, Capernaum is one of several ancient fishing villages on the Sea of Galilee. To its northeast is Bethsaida, to the south is Magdala. Across the sea is Susita, Aramaic for Hippos, one of the cities of the Decapolis. Because of its designation as the hometown of Jesus, archaeological inquiries began as early as 1838, when American scholar Edward Robinson identified a synagogue among the ruins.[1] The Franciscans purchased two-thirds of the site in 1846; the remaining third is held by the Greek Orthodox patriarchate.

The results of various archaeological endeavors have created a snapshot of what first-century Capernaum looked like. Probably a few rows of houses skirted the shore, allowing fishermen easy access to the water. No large structures dating to the first century were discovered, but underneath the fifth-century limestone synagogue, the foundation of black basalt stones are visible. Since most sanctuaries were built on top of preexisting ones, archaeologists surmise that the current visible structure stands on top of a synagogue of the first century.

The synagogue overlooks exposed courtyards of basalt stone organized in an irregular pattern. Beyond this first series of homes, another courtyard is visible under a modern church built by the Franciscans.

[1] John J. Rousseau and Rami Arav, *Jesus and His World* (Minneapolis: Fortress, 1995) 40.

The modern church was built above an earlier structure, the origins of which date back to the first century. This room originally served as a home, with pottery evidencing domestic use until the mid-first century. After that the walls were plastered, and only storage jars and lamps were found. Given the relative poverty of the surrounding homes at that time, plastered walls would indicate a structure of prominence and value.

Visiting Capernaum between 381 and 384, the pilgrim Egeria noted: "In Capernaum the house of the prince of the apostles has been made into a church, with its original walls still standing. . . . There also is the synagogue where the Lord cured a man possessed by the devil."[2] Graffiti scratched into the plaster speak of Jesus as Lord and Christ, and archaeological evidence seems to support Egeria's report that by the fourth century a house church with a central arch occupied this space. A century later an octagonal church was built over the site, with the central octagon enshrining the venerated room.

Following the Constantinian period, when Christianity became the legitimate religion of the Roman Empire, "holy" sites and venerated spots became numerous. The house church in Capernaum witnessed to a longer history of veneration, beginning shortly after the death of Jesus. While it is impossible to know for certain who the original owner was, there is no archaeological evidence to contradict that this may indeed have been the house of St. Peter.

Reflection

The sea is still in the early morning. Few tourists have arrived. The archaeological ruins of Capernaum lie silent under the bright sun. Violet and pink bougainvillea wave long arms in the soft breeze. Set up against the water's edge, Capernaum still captures the Christian imagination. While pilgrims are often dismayed and disappointed that Jerusalem grew up and dressed in modern buildings and twentieth-century ways, they are soothed by Capernaum's coy appearance. Nearly two thousand years after a craftsman from Nazareth relocated to this fishing village, Capernaum has changed little.

While the fifth-century synagogue draws attention with its limestone façade, it is the nearness of the lake that is striking. The site reverenced as the house of Peter is barely fifty yards from the water's edge. The synagogue may have been Capernaum's religious center, but surely the sea was its economic base. Clinging to its banks, Capernaum, like Bethsaida to its northeast, provided fishermen like Peter,

[2] Jerome Murphy-O'Connor, O.P., *The Holy Land* (New York: Oxford University Press, 1992) 224.

The synagogue of Capernaum rises above the first-century basalt-stone village.

Andrew, James, and John with a steady business, though archaeological evidence from the first century indicates that the homes were poor and the community small.

The fishing industry provided the town with an economy burdened by heavy taxation. "Fishermen leased their fishing rights from persons called 'toll collectors' in the New Testament for a percentage of the catch. Evidence indicates that such lease fees could run as high as 40 percent."[3] Perhaps the first disciples of Jesus—Peter, Andrew, James, and John—were fishermen who were heavily taxed. Many Gospel stories center on this fishing industry. Peter is called while fishing (Luke 5:1-11). James and John leave their father's fishing business (Mark 1:16-20). After Jesus' crucifixion the disciples return to Galilee and spend a night fishing (John 21:1-14). The boats used for fishing at night become the platform for preaching in the day (Luke 5:3) and transportation across the water to other villages (Mark 4:35; 6:54). The sea, fishing, boats, and fishermen with their harbor village at Capernaum become the anchor for Jesus' ministry.

When Jesus adopts Capernaum as his hometown, he joins its first-century community. He worships in its synagogue (Mark 1:21), resides

[3] Bruce Malina and Richard Rohrbaugh, *Social-Science Commentary on the Synoptic Gospels* (Minneapolis: Fortress, 1992) 44.

with or near Peter (Mark 2:1), heals its residents (Mark 1:30-31), and assists in its fishing industry (Luke 5:4). While Jesus works as an itinerant preacher, Capernaum serves as his home base, and much of his teaching occurs within a three-mile radius. Jerome Murphy-O'Connor, commenting on the archaeological evidences of first-century Capernaum, notes: "No unique advantages induced Jesus to settle there; it offered nothing that could not be found in the other lakeside towns. He probably chose it because his first converts, the fishermen Peter and Andrew, lived there (Mark 1:21, 29)."[4]

Since 1335, during the rule of the Mamluk dynasty, the Franciscans have made the Holy Land their home. Serving as the guardians of "Terra Sancta," they have become its priests, gatekeepers, archaeologists, and caretakers. Each Franciscan province sends friars to the Holy Land. At Capernaum their friary stands just inside the gate, announcing "The Hometown of Jesus." While thousands of pilgrims pass by the basalt stone building, few have reason or interest to enter. More often the Franciscans are seen as the guardians of modesty and keepers of the keys to the Church of St. Peter.

Yet on one occasion a furtive knock at the friary brought Father Pedro quickly to the door. A young tourist was ill and asked to rest there while her tour group visited the site. As one at home with urgent requests for healing and help, he opened the parlor, threw back the shade, and invited the guest to rest for awhile. One cannot help but think of another Pedro (Peter) who long ago watched a preacher take the hand of his mother-in-law and heal her. The message of Capernaum does not lie in its interesting archaeology or lapping shore but in the insight that home and healing are gifts to be shared.

---

[4] Murphy-O'Connor, *The Holy Land,* 223.

The Church of the Sermon on the Mount is surrounded by lush gardens and has a commanding view of the sea.

12. The Mount of Beatitudes

Scripture Readings

About the Site

Land speaks in many ways. Land may be silent and rugged, creating a harsh and unfriendly challenge to survival. Or land may be a willing dialogue partner, welcoming people to settle permanently by providing the source for food and livelihood. The area of Israel/Palestine known as Galilee is the garden next to the Judean desert. The name Galilee means "circle" and refers to a district or region that stretches about forty miles from north to south (from the north end of the Plain of Esdraelon to Dan), and twenty-five miles from east to west (from the Mediterranean coast to the rift valley including the Sea of Galilee and the upper reaches of the Jordan River).

An east-west fault line running from Acco on the coast to just north of the Sea of Galilee divides the area into upper and lower Galilee. The terrain of upper Galilee differs significantly from that of lower Galilee. Upper Galilee is dominated by rugged mountains. The area has been "a haven from political and religious persecution, an environment for hermits, bandits and colonies of purist religious observance."[1] Lower Galilee is marked by alternating hills and plains on an east-west axis. The hills and valleys range in height from five hundred feet above sea level to seven hundred feet below. Water running from the hillsides creates a fertile alluvial soil on the floor of the basins between the hills. Towns climb up the hillsides and flocks are pastured there; the valleys between are used for agriculture. Josephus describes the plains of Galilee as

[1] Anne Hennessy, C.S.J., *The Galilee of Jesus* (Rome: Editrice Pontificia Universita Gregoriana, 1994) 9.

a region whose natural properties and beauty are very remarkable. There is not a plant which its fertile soil refuses to produce,
and its cultivator in fact grows every species; the air is so well-
tempered that it suits the most opposite varieties. The walnut, a
tree which delights in the most wintry climate, here grows luxuri-
antly, beside palm trees, which thrive on heat, and figs and olives,
which require a milder atmosphere. One might say that nature
had taken pride in thus assembling, by a *tour de force,* the most dis-
cordant species in a single spot, and that, by a happy rivalry, each
of the seasons wished to claim this region for its own.[2]

Narrow corridors between hills are used as roads. One of these corridors was a main highway in ancient times and was used for camel
trains as late as the nineteenth century. This path is also the direct road
between Nazareth, passing by Cana to the Sea of Galilee near Capernaum, a distance of approximately twenty miles. According to a firsthand description written by Colonel Sir Charles Wilson, a royal
engineer in the British army and one of the foremost explorers of Palestine in the 1860s, "the path is neither rough nor difficult, and, as we de-
scend, the cliffs rise higher and higher on either hand, and we perceive
that the walls of rock are perforated with holes. This is called Wadi el
Hamam, or the Valley of the Doves, and myriads of them make their
home in these rocks."[3] At the end of the Valley of the Doves, at the foot
of Mount Arbel, the traveler would reach the city of Magdala on the
coast of the Sea of Galilee and along the Via Maris. Three miles north
of Magdala is Heptapegon, the fishing ground of Capernaum's fishermen. Heptapegon in Greek means "seven springs," and was shortened
by Arab tongues to Tabgha. The warm springs here attract fish, especially in winter.

The hardy pilgrim Egeria wrote an extensive account of her three
years of travel in the lands of the Bible (381–384). She describes the
area and the tradition surrounding Tabgha and the Mount of the Beatitudes in these words:

> Not far away from there [Capernaum] there are some stone steps
> where the Lord stood. And in the same place by the sea is a grassy
> field with plenty of land and many palm trees. By them are seven
> springs, each flowing strongly. And this is the field where the Lord

[2] Josephus, *The Jewish War,* III, 10, 8, par. 516-521, as quoted in Jack Finegan, *The Archaeology of the New Testament* (Princeton, N.J.: Princeton University Press, 1992) 83.

[3] W. Wilson, *The Land of Galilee* (Jerusalem: Ariel, 1976) 68; reprinted from the book originally published in 1880 under the title *Picturesque Palestine.*

fed the people with the five loaves and the two fishes. The stone on which the Lord placed the bread has been made into an altar. . . . Along the walls of the church runs the public highway where the apostle Matthew sat to collect taxes. On the hill which rises nearby is a grotto, upon which the Lord ascended when he taught the Beatitudes.[4]

This hill, today called the Mount of the Beatitudes, is craggy and has probably always been left uncultivated. It is tranquil and beautiful, inviting a quiet contemplation of the waters below. From its crest one can see all the places where Jesus lived and worked. In the springtime the hills of Galilee are green and lush with a profusion of flowers in a riot of glorious color. As Bargil Pixner writes, "The human heart expands in response to such beauty. It must have been the red anemones and the blue iris that inspired Jesus to reflect on the lilies of the field (Matt 6:28) whose beauty surpasses that of Solomon's in all its splendor (Matt 6:29)."[5]

Reflection

Scholars agree that this first of five discourses in the Gospel of Matthew (5:1–7:29) and the Lukan parallel (6:20-49) are each created by their authors from a collection of sayings of Jesus. No one knows if a crowd of five thousand people, "not counting the women and children," gathered at a particular spot along the northwest side of the Sea of Galilee to hear Jesus preach. Yet over the centuries a steady stream of pilgrims and a few archaeologists have focused on one specific location where the likelihood of this kind of gathering is plausible. As early as the fourth century, Egeria mentions her visit to the place where Jesus spoke the Beatitudes. Interestingly, the site to which she refers fits the details of different descriptions given by Matthew and Luke. In Matthew the sermon is delivered from a mountain (5:1), while in Luke, Jesus speaks on a level plain (6:17). Both a hill and a plain are located here just above the seven springs of Tabgha.

Volumes have been, and will continue to be, written on the content of Jesus' sermon. The truth as spoken through the Word of God continues to be revealed as our lives change and different circumstances bring deeper levels of understanding. This brief reflection is focused on the setting of these Gospel readings. The land of Israel/Palestine is called by some a "fifth gospel," because the setting in which the message is

---

[4] John Wilkinson, *Egeria's Travels to the Holy Land* (Jerusalem: Ariel, 1981) 196.
[5] Bargil Pixner, O.S.B., *With Jesus Through Galilee According to the Fifth Gospel* (Rosh Pina, Israel: Corazin, 1992) 37.

given contributes as much to the revelation as the words themselves. To know the *place* is itself revelatory. One's whole self becomes more fully engaged in the event as every single sense comes alive. The same could be said of a special meal or the memory of a significant moment: the setting in which the event takes place contributes significantly to its meaning for us.

Carroll Stuhlmueller, C.P., describes the Sermon on the Mount in Matthew's Gospel (beginning with Matthew 5:1) as a grand opening![6] The end of chapter 4 summarizes Jesus' missionary program (4:23). Chapters 5, 6, and 7 and the parallel sayings in Luke are a bold, daring, and radical pronouncement about an abrupt change in the history of Israel—a new Moses, a different perspective on the Hebrew Scriptures, a call to a change of heart, a new way of life full of promises for the future as well as some benefits now. For this grand proclamation, Jesus uses simple language and images that would be commonly understood by his listeners because they reflect the realities of Galilean life. Jesus' message would not have been as clear or as well received if it had been delivered in Jerusalem.

A ten-minute walk from the place where Jesus was preaching was the commercial port city of Magdala, which is probably the Tarichaea mentioned by Josephus. Tarchae means "dried fish." The industry here was the salting and shipping of dried fish. Jars and barrels of fish were carried by caravan to Syria or sent overland to Ptolemais (Acco) and then shipped west. "You are the salt of the earth. But if salt loses its taste, with what can it be seasoned?" (Matt 5:13). Salt is an image that would have been instantly understood by fisherman, merchant, homemaker, or anyone listening who had brought along a picnic lunch.

Susita (Hippos) was a Greek city, part of the Decapolis with a port on the eastern side of the lake across from Tarichaea. The city center was built up high so that it could be seen from all points of the lake.[7] "You are the light of the world. A city set on a mountain cannot be hidden" (Matt 5:14). Jesus could see Susita in the distance across the lake from where he was preaching. His listeners, with a turn of the head, could see it too.

The Jews in Galilee lived in the midst of pagans (Gentiles). Canaanites, Phoenicians, Samaritans, Greeks, and Romans lived in a mixed population, especially in the larger cities of Sepphoris and Tiberias. Observant Jews would be distinguished in dress and lifestyle from the

---

[6] Carroll Stuhlmueller, C.P., *Biblical Meditations for Ordinary Time* (Ramsey, N.J.: Paulist Press, 1984) 257.

[7] Hennessy, *The Galilee of Jesus*, 46.

The Mount of Beatitudes begins with a steep climb from the water's edge and then tapers to a gradual incline.

non-Jews with whom they might do business. The pagan, foreigner, or stranger could not be trusted and so was considered an enemy. "You have heard that it was said, 'You shall love your neighbor and hate your enemy.' But I say to you, love your enemies . . ." (Matt 5:43-44). This challenge to a change of heart would have had an immediate and disturbing impact on Jewish societal attitudes that had been ingrained for generations.

Lower Galilee has an abundance of both local and migratory birds. Kingfishers, egrets, bulburs, crows, woodpeckers, wrens, and sparrows are a common sight throughout the year.[8] "Look at the birds in the sky; they do not sow or reap, they gather nothing into barns, yet your heavenly Father feeds them" (Matt 6:26). In the springtime wild flowers cover the hills of Galilee. Their bright, colorful beauty is fragile and fleeting. "Why are you anxious about clothes? Learn from the way the wild flowers grow. They do not work or spin. But I tell you

[8] Ibid.

that not even Solomon in all his splendor was clothed like one of them. . . . Will [God] not much more provide for you?" (Matt 6:28-30).

Salt, light, neighbor, birds, wild flowers, a grassy hillside, a sparkling lake are all material aspects of the landscape and daily lives of the people of Galilee. These images become the symbols that embody the message: *you* are the salt, *you* are the light. The birds and the wild flowers are images that become symbols of a compassionate, loving God who is both father and mother to us. It is in this way that the land speaks and the setting of the Gospel message contributes to the revelation of the words themselves. In our reflection on the Scriptures, these images will only become symbols of God's love for us if we discover their meaning in our own lives. It is not enough to recall what these images meant for someone living in first-century Galilee. We have to make them live today.

At the base of the hill, the village of Nain (Nein in Hebrew) is surrounded by fields of roses.

13. Nain

Scripture Reading

Cycle C   10th Sunday of Ordinary Time   Luke 7:11-17

About the Site

The Nain in Luke's Gospel is a village identified with modern Nein, six miles southeast of Nazareth at the foot of Givat Hamoreh in the Valley of Jezreel. Later Jewish sources claim that the town's name in Hebrew means "pleasant." With a view of Mount Tabor to the northeast and of Nazareth to the northwest, the village was located on the Via Maris, on the route from Sepphoris to Beth Shean (Scythopolis).[1] Its position on this major Roman thoroughfare, along with the presence of a spring, would have made Nain a village of some prominence. A reference is made to a city gate in Luke 7:12, but the village was never fortified, so there was no gate in the proper sense of the word. "Gate" may refer to the place where the road entered between the houses. Ruins of a medieval church are visible in the village, and to the southeast are ancient rock-cut tombs used during the first century.

Reflection

After healing the slave of the centurion in Capernaum (Luke 7:1-10), Jesus, his disciples, and a large crowd journey to Nain, a small village about twenty-one miles southwest of Capernaum. As Jesus and his crowd approach, they are met by another group leaving the village with a body to be buried. When Jesus sees the widow who has lost her only son, he is moved with pity. The focus of the story is not the dead son but the suffering widow.

Luke favors widows in his Gospel: the widow Anna in the Temple, who "spoke about the child to all who were awaiting the redemption of Jerusalem" (Luke 2:38); the persistent widow who continually petitioned the unjust judge (Luke 18:1-5); the widow who "from her poverty offered her whole livelihood" (Luke 21:4) to the Temple treasury. Widows in first-century Israel received no inheritance rights and often had to rely on public charity to survive. "Widowhood was perceived by some to be a disgrace; death before old age was probably

[1] John J. Rousseau and Rami Arav, *Jesus and His World* (Minneapolis: Fortress, 1995) 213.

viewed as a judgment upon sin, and the reproach extended to the sur-
viving spouse" (Ruth 1:19-21; Isa 54:4).[2]

Understanding the bleak situation of this widow from Nain, Jesus
stops the procession and touches the coffin, an act that would render
him unclean. "Young man, I tell you, arise!" (Luke 7:14). The young
man is brought back to life and given to his mother, in an act reminiscent of 1 Kings 17:23 and 2 Kings 4:32-37. So similar is this event to the
raising of the dead by Elijah and Elisha that the crowds exclaim, "A
great prophet has arisen in our midst" (Luke 7:16). Luke explains that
this report spread throughout the whole of Judea, an interesting fact,
considering that Nain was located in the southeast corner of Galilee
and not Judea. However, in 4:44 Luke says that Jesus "was preaching
in the synagogues of Judea," though certainly he is still in Galilee.
Other manuscripts read "Galilee"; hence, the Gospel writer probably
means the land of Israel and not the political entity of Judea.

After Jesus' miracle, he is questioned by the disciples of John the
Baptist. Since the Gospel of John has the Baptist at Aenon, twenty
miles or so southeast of Nain, one could surmise that the news of the
widow's son spread quickly. "Are you the one who is to come, or
should we look for another?" (Luke 7:19), the disciples of John are sent
to ask. In a world expecting a messiah, all disciples look for hope. Jesus
presents a very different image: "Go and tell John what you have seen
and heard: the blind regain their sight, the lame walk, lepers are
cleansed, the deaf hear, the dead are raised, the poor have the good
news proclaimed to them" (Luke 7:22). Jesus brings healing to the sick
and restores those who are outcasts from the community. More important, Jesus offers this freely and to the least among them. The widow
of Nain, mourning the loss of both her son and her status in the community, did not ask for help. On the contrary, it was Jesus who stopped
the funeral procession. It was Jesus who entered into the grief, moved
with pity; it was Jesus who risked his own "status" to give the woman
back her connection with the community, her security, her son. The
weeping widow of Nain foreshadows another widow at the foot of the
cross; only then it will be God who enters into the passion, stops the
procession of death, and restores hope to the broken hearts.

The modern-day village of Nain is tucked neatly against the hillside, with a wide slice of the Jezreel stretching before it. In fields that
spread like an apron in front of the town, rows of roses bloom. And
somewhere southeast of the city ancient tombs lie silent, stone witnesses to a funeral procession robbed of death.

---

[2] Paul Achtemeier, ed., *Harper's Bible Dictionary* (San Francisco: Harper & Row,
1985) 1132.

Where the southern end of the Plain of Gennesaret meets the Sea of Galilee, the thriving city of Magdala stood. In the background are the outskirts of Tiberias.

14. Magdala

Scripture Reading

Cycle C   11th Sunday of Ordinary Time   Luke 7:36–8:3

About the Site

Strategically located, ancient Magdala sat at the junction of the road to Tiberias three miles south, and the Via Maris to its west. A few miles northward lay Capernaum and the toll booth to the tetrarchy of Philip. The city was known by several names: Tarichaea, meaning "salted fish" in Greek; Migdal, meaning "tower" or "fortress" in Hebrew; and Migdal Nunaiya, meaning "fish tower" in Hebrew. As most of the names indicate, the local fish economy provided the city with wealth, while its location allowed for trade. Magdala sat at the edge of the Sea of Galilee, with the Plain of Gennesaret stretching north behind it. According to first-century Jewish historian Josephus, the city sported a hippodrome, evidencing its Greek character.

Archaeological excavations in the 1970s uncovered a Roman city plan with a cardo maximus running north and south, intersected by an east-west decuman gate (the main entrance of a Roman army camp, so named for the tenth cohort of the legion, usually camped there[1]). Pottery and coins found in a synagogue date the structure between the late Hellenistic and early Roman period. It was probably destroyed during the First Jewish Revolt (66–73), when the Romans laid siege to Magdala. According to Josephus, forty thousand people lived in the city at the time of the siege, and many fled in boats. The Romans pursued the Jews on makeshift rafts, and the battle that ensued left the waters of the lake red with blood. A mosaic now on display at Capernaum shows one of the boats at Magdala.

Magdala is known as the home of Mary, a disciple of Jesus from whom seven demons were cast out (Luke 8:2). The Gospels also refer to it as Magadan (Matt 15:39) and Dalmanutha (Mark 8:10), the latter simply being another name for the same place.[2]

---

[1] Jack Finegan, *The Archaeology of the New Testament* (Princeton, N.J.: Princeton University Press, 1992) 82.

[2] Ibid., 81.

Reflection

A small sign indicates "Magdala Beach" and points down a dirt road. Beyond the palms and banana groves, a rocky beach opens up and follows a narrow strip of land southward. On Sabbath afternoons the beach is filled with families picnicking and swimming. An Arab woman in a long dress sits in the water, with her children splashing nearby. Modesty prevents her from exposing all but her hands and face. She seems unencumbered by her soggy attire. Behind her a young woman clad in a tiny bikini walks by, and once again Magdala is filled with women of contradiction.

This Sunday's reading from the Gospel of Luke is a story of women. The first one is a woman "who loved much." Moved by her experience of being healed by Jesus, she washes his feet with her tears and dries them with her hair. The ensuing conversation between Jesus and his host, Simon, a Pharisee, presents a portrait of first-century hospitality.

The second group of women were followers of Jesus who "provided for [Jesus and the Twelve] out of their resources" (Luke 8:3). Interestingly the word for "provide" is a form of *diakonia*, "service," and is the word Jesus will use to describe his own ministry at the Last Supper. Though it was unusual for women to travel outside their immediate homes, some women did support rabbis and traveled with their entourage. However, given that most of Jesus' preaching was within a few miles of Capernaum, the women could have returned home at night. Magdala, for example, is less than five miles from Capernaum. Joanna's husband, Chuza, Herod's steward, would have lived in Tiberias, then the capital.[3] Tiberias is less than ten miles from Capernaum, certainly a manageable walk in a day.

That these three women had some financial wherewithal indicates a certain level of independence. Only Joanna's husband is named. Mary is known by her town, perhaps to distinguish her from other Marys who were part of this group or to indicate that she was not married. The text adds that there were "many others," leading us to believe that the number of women followers was significant.

The Jewish women followers of Jesus have strong sisters today who shoulder their share of the burden of building a country on the edge of conflict. Civan is nineteen years old and in a year will finish her military duty. At eighteen years of age every Jewish woman must spend two years in the army,[4] and though she may not have to serve on the front lines, she is required to carry a rifle nearly bigger than she is.

[3] John E. Stambaugh and David L. Balch, *The New Testament in Its Social Environment*, ed. Wayne A. Meeks (Philadelphia: Westminster, 1986) 103.

[4] At eighteen, Jewish men must spend three years in the military.

While their Jewish counterparts are charging through bootcamp exercises in one-hundred-degree heat, the Arab women of the Old City seem more than miles apart. And indeed, since the Intifada, many of them have returned to a more conservative dress, covering all but their faces and hands. A casual observer might think that this is a step back from modernism and feminism. That would be too quick a judgment. Many Muslim women who reappropriated modest dress did so, not out of strict observance, but out of solidarity and witness. They were reclaiming their identity through their dress. Suddenly there seemed to be more Muslims simply because they began to dress distinctly.

But when her shift is over, Civan wears jeans and t-shirts and is happier listening to Tracy Chapman than marching drills. Just over the hills from Civan's family home in Timrat, the minaret begins the call to prayer, and in the nearby Bedouin village other nineteen-year-old girls stop their work, cover their heads, and begin to pray.

Windsurfers now favor the narrow natural harbor probably used by Jesus when he preached from the boat.

15. Preaching in a Boat on the Sea

Scripture Readings

Cycle A	15–17th Sundays of Ordinary Time	Matt 13:1-52
Cycle B	11th Sunday of Ordinary Time	Mark 4:26-34
Cycle C	3rd Sunday of Easter	John 21:1-19

About the Site

A little more than a mile south of Capernaum is Tabgha, remembered as the site where Jesus multiplied the loaves and fishes. "Et-Tabgha" is an Arabic corruption of the Greek "Heptapegon," meaning "seven springs." Indeed, many springs gush forth on a little plain built up by the silt from Wadi ed-Jamus, which descends to the lake at this point. Outcroppings of black basalt and limestone rock made the area poor for farming in the first century, but the presence of the springs emptying into the sea supported good fishing. In fact, remembered here also is the post-resurrection fishing account of Jesus meeting the disciples on the shore (John 21:1-14).

In the fourth century a Byzantine church was built to commemorate the site. Only a few walls remain and are encompassed within the Franciscan chapel built in 1933. Along the shore beside the church, six heart-shaped stones stretch into the lake. Their position suggests a colonnade, but their original use is unknown. They are first mentioned in a text in the year 808 and were known as the Twelve Thrones, commemorating the apostles.[1]

Of this site Jack Finegan writes, "While Tabgha was itself secluded, it was close enough to farms and villages that people could run there on foot from the villages and get there before Jesus, coming by boat (Mark 6:33), and the disciples could suggest going to farms and villages round about to buy food (Mark 6:36)."[2]

A half mile north of Tabgha the Mount of Beatitudes descends sharply into the sea. The angle of descent and the presence of an inlet at the water's edge create a natural amphitheater. No archaeological

---

[1] Jerome Murphy-O'Connor, O.P., *The Holy Land* (New York: Oxford University Press, 1992) 288.

[2] Jack Finegan, *The Archaeology of the New Testament* (Princeton, N.J.: Princeton University Press, 1992) 87.

evidence supports this as the site where Jesus taught the crowds from the boat, but topography does. If one stands at the bottom by the shore, those standing some hundred yards up can hear clearly.

Reflection

Once unsuited for farming, the base of the Mount of Beatitudes though still littered with huge basalt stones is now a field of watermelons. The hill declines sharply beyond the road and ends at a natural inlet. Today windsurfers use the inlet as a safe harbor for setting up their sails. On a holiday or Sabbath afternoon, hundreds of sails dot the water. The only other boats on the sea are the "Jesus Boats," which resemble vessels from the first century. Their catch of the day is tourists, who crowd aboard to have an "authentic" trip across the Sea of Galilee. The fishers are long gone by the time windsurfers and tourists arrive, preferring the pre-dawn hours for the best fishing. The Saint Peter's Fish (Tilapia Galilea), carp, and freshwater sardine are most often their catch.

As one sits above the inlet on the steep hill, it is easy to think about that prophetic Rabbi who spoke in parables about things the locals could understand: wheat and weeds, mustard seeds and yeast—common, everyday parts of an ordinary life. Perhaps part of the power of Jesus was his ability to use the land and its resources to reflect the image of God.

The Eremos Cave at the base of the Mount of Beatitudes creates a quiet space for reflection and contemplation.

16. A Deserted Place

About the Site

First-century Galilee was not a quiet place. The Via Maris passed along a section of the west side of the Sea of Galilee from Mount Arbel heading north through Capernaum, Bethsaida, and then eastward to Damascus. This international highway was a major passage for commerce between Egypt and Mesopotamia. Armies marched along this road; caravans with thousands of camels burdened with goods were a common sight. Agriculture flourished. Josephus says, perhaps with some exaggeration, that "the towns, too, are thickly distributed, and even the villages, thanks to the fertility of the soil, are all so densely populated that the smallest of them contains above fifteen thousand inhabitants."[1]

Despite the dense population and busy highway, the geography of Galilee provides many opportunities for seclusion and quiet. The mountains of Upper Galilee afford an accessible place to be alone (Luke 9:18). The alternating hills and plains of Lower Galilee are separated by wadis, narrow corridors where water drains from the hillsides toward the Sea of Galilee. The wadis are pockmarked with caves and, especially in the lush spring and summer seasons, cool streams and thick vegetation provide privacy in a setting of natural beauty.

The fishing towns of Capernaum and Bethsaida were important centers of Jesus' ministry. Near these villages the lakeshore was separated from the farming area by a mound called Tel Orimeh, an ancient Phoenician outpost, and a rocky stretch of shoreline, a perfect "lonely place." From these rocks come seven springs, which today give the

---

[1] Jack Finegan, *The Archaeology of the New Testament* (Princeton, N.J.: Princeton University Press, 1992) 76.

area its name, Tabgha.[2] In the rainy season grass sprouts in the shallow layer of soil on the rocky hills (John 6:4, 10). The plain of the Seven Springs (Tabgha) is associated by tradition with several Gospel events, among them the feeding of the five thousand (Matt 14:13-21; Mark 6:30-44; John 6:1-13).

Excavations in this area by Bellarmino Bagatti in 1968 show that ruined watertowers used as part of an irrigation project date from the fourth century. In the early second century, there was a stone quarry here. But in Gospel times Tabgha was a secluded, unused area, not suited for farming and not the site of a village. As such, this area corresponds well with the description "a deserted place" (Mark 6:31). Tabgha is close to the lakeshore (Mark 6:32), and there are hills close by (John 6:3, 15). Nearby is a small cave referred to as Eremos. The cave is up the hill from the sea, nestled under an overhang that is part of the Mount of Beatitudes. The interior of the cave is not large, but it is sufficient to provide shelter for several people; it faces the sea, allowing a spectacular view of land, water, and sky.

Egeria referred to this cave, "Eremos, a deserted place," as the place of the Sermon on the Beatitudes.[3] A multitude would not have fit in this cave, but some commentators believe that the sermon was delivered to a few disciples and not to crowds. In any case, the cave is a secluded place with protection from the sun and heat during the day. It is adequate in size for five or six people to gather. Its large opening would allow a full view of the sea and the night sky. The Gospels suggest that Jesus often went "up on the mountain" to pray (Matt 14:23; Mark 6:46). This cave is a good example of the kind of place Jesus may have chosen for prayer. Today, in the midst of busloads of pilgrims visiting the sites below, this cave is still accessible. It is just far enough away from the crowds to be secluded and quiet.

While Tabgha itself was secluded, it was close to farms and villages. When Jesus withdrew by boat to go to a deserted place to pray, local people traveling on foot could get to the shore first in order to be there when he arrived (Mark 6:33; Matt 14:13). The close proximity of dense population also supports the disciples' suggestion to "go and buy food for all these people" (Luke 9:13) or to "dismiss the crowds so that they can go to the villages and buy food for themselves" (Matt 14:15). One who knew the land well could always find a quiet place in the mountains, wadis, or along the lakeshore to pray, to be alone with friends, or to preach to a large crowd.

---

[2] Heptapegon is a Greek word meaning "seven springs." The Arabic tongue shortened the name to Tabgha.

[3] John Wilkinson, *Egeria's Travels to the Holy Land* (Jerusalem: Ariel, 1981) 200.

Reflection

Because the word "desert" forms part of the phrase "a deserted place," one may imagine Jesus going to a barren place, devoid of life, perhaps even dangerous because of its isolation. These descriptions do not fit any location in Galilee. Galilee is fertile everywhere. The "deserted place" or "lonely place" would be a place away from people. Even though one could withdraw from the busyness of crowds and industry, usually the distance was so short that activity could still be seen and perhaps heard. The hills of Galilee or the steep sides of a wadi can surround one with the peace and refreshment that are the gifts of nature. Uninhabited stretches of lakeshore, untouched by the fishing industry of the day, would be devoid of human activity but teeming with the life cycle of plants and animals. To seek such a place to pray is to seek the God of all creation. Jesus left the complex social world of Galilee to meet his God in solitude and then used examples from the natural landscape consistently in his teaching.

What happened in the "deserted places" where Jesus went to pray? Amazingly, the places are far from deserted. In Matthew 14:13-21 and Mark 6:30-34, though Jesus attempts to be alone after hearing of the death of John, crowds follow him. His heart goes out to them; he cures their sick and feeds them until thousands have eaten their fill. Even the leftovers are abundant. In Luke 9:18-24 and 11:1-13, Jesus does not find thousands waiting for him, but he is not alone. His disciples are with him. In these two readings the exchange between Jesus and his disciples in their quiet time together is quite profound.

In Luke 9:18 Jesus asks his disciples, "Who do the crowds say that I am?" In their response it is Peter, destined for leadership among the disciples, who acknowledges, "The Messiah of God" (9:20). This exchange marks a deepening of the relationship between Jesus and his small band of companions. As their understanding of Jesus and his mission grows, he begins to reveal to them the depth of commitment required for discipleship. It is in this setting of intimate conversation that he tells them, "Whoever wishes to save his life will lose it, but whoever loses his life for my sake will save it" (Luke 9:24).

It is in a similar setting that the disciples ask Jesus to teach them to pray (Luke 11:1). The words of the prayer Jesus teaches them are now the most common prayer known to all Christians. The significance of this prayer goes beyond the vertical relationship with God the Father. What Jesus teaches them includes new dimensions of fatherhood within their own society. "Ask and you will receive; seek and you will find; knock and the door will be opened to you" (Luke 11:9). It is the obligation of the father, the head of the household, not only to provide sustenance but to be generous, to be the source of abundance for the family. This abundance is not meant in terms of material wealth but in the realm of the aesthetic, that which is beautiful and delightful.[4] "If you then, who are wicked, know how to give good gifts to your children, how much more will the Father in heaven give the holy Spirit to those who ask him?" (11:13). Perhaps this perspective of fatherhood with loving care was learned from contemplating the abundance and beauty of creation along the lakeshore and in the wadis of Galilee.

In the reading from John's Gospel (John 6:1-15), Jesus' search for a deserted place comes after an encounter with a crowd. In their exuberant gratitude for the miraculous feeding that has just taken place, the crowd wants to make Jesus king. He flees to a quiet place not only to avoid their misguided (though understandable) intentions but to contemplate this experience of the power of God within him.

In each of these gospel readings the deserted place is not deserted! Perhaps the "deserted place" is meant to be a place away from the ordinary, a place where one can be nurtured by creation, by friendship, by food, by prayer, by becoming focused again. Time spent in prayer prepares one to be with and for the people of God.

---

[4] Anne Hennessy, C.S.J., *The Galilee of Jesus* (Rome: Editrice Pontificia Universita Gregoriana, 1994) 34–35.

The Sea of Galilee has many moods, from morning calms to afternoon tantrums. But after sudden storms, the water quiets, even sparkles, in the fading light.

17. Walking on the Water

Scripture Reading

Cycle A   19th Sunday of Ordinary Time   Matt 14:22-33

About the Site

The Sea of Galilee, 670 feet below sea level, surrounded on three sides by mountains, is subject to sudden and violent storms. Strong gusts of wind coming from the surrounding wadis can change the surface of the sea from tranquil to tumultuous in a matter of minutes. A cold east wind, the Sharkiyeh, comes up suddenly, particularly during the winter season, and can be harsh and dangerous.[1] Though the sea is only seven miles wide at its broadest point, the wind raises waves large enough to engulf an open boat of the size used by fishermen in the first century. Waves arrive at one shore only to be thrown back into a fierce collision with the next wave rolling in. Those in the fishing industry who work at night dread this wind because it is impossible to sail or row against it. The sudden storms can be life threatening even for the experienced seafarer.

Another factor affecting the conditions of maneuvering on the sea is the effect of the Jordan River. The Jordan enters the sea at the north end and exits at the south, providing a current in this small body of water. The disciples heading northeast from Tabgha toward Bethsaida by boat would have been rowing against both the current and the wind.

Reflection

This gospel reading is about faith and power. The land provides the background for this episode in the developing ministry of Jesus and how his closest disciples understood him. It is in personal prayer, particularly in contact with nature, that one becomes aware of the power of God. From the vantage point of a cave with a sufficiently large opening to see the sky, Jesus could contemplate the beauty of creation all around him. To be alone in prayer in the midst of a mountain covered with delicate wildflowers, a sparkling sea filled with a variety and abundance of fish, the night sky brimming over with stars is to be embraced by the love and delight of the Creator. The beauty of the

[1] Bargil Pixner, O.S.B., *With Jesus Through Galilee* (Rosh Pina, Israel: Corazin, 1992) 74.

Eremos cave and its surroundings perhaps filled Jesus with a sense of awe best expressed by the psalmist:

> When I see your heavens, the work of your fingers,
>> the moon and stars that you set in place—
> What are humans that you are mindful of them,
>> mere mortals that you care for them?
> Yet you have made them little less than a god,
>> crowned them with glory and honor.
> You have given them rule over the works of your hand,
>> put all things at their feet (Ps 8:4-7).

As the hours passed and daylight faded, a strong gusty wind came up, bringing about a dangerous storm on the sea. This image, too, tells of the strength and power of God, not in the same way as the gentle beauty of creation but as something to overcome. The power of the Creator to control raging waters is sung throughout the psalms:

> You still the roaring of the seas,
>> the roaring of their waves,
>> the tumult of the peoples (Ps 65:8).[2]

The image of waters that surge, roar, and swell, bringing great peril to those caught in them, is an image used to describe chaos and rebellion among the people. Jesus had just learned of the violent murder of John the Baptist (Matt 14:12). When he tried to be alone with his disciples to mourn the loss of John, crowds followed him (Matt 14:13). He cured their sick and fed them (Matt 14:13-21). Now he is finally alone with time to reflect on these events. The storm arising on the sea, with its harsh winds and crashing waves, might have symbolized for Jesus the forces of evil that brought about John's death and the chaos of the crowds that surrounded him during the day. It is only God who has the power to calm this kind of storm.

> The flood has raised up, LORD,
>> the flood has raised up its roar;
>> the flood has raised its pounding waves.
> More powerful than the roar of many waters,
>> more powerful than the breakers of the sea,
>> powerful in the heavens is the LORD (Ps 93:4).

In the context of prayer, bringing with him the events of the recent past and with a growing concern over the safety of his disciples, Jesus came to know that the power of God to calm these waters was within him.

---

[2] See also Psalms 89:10; 93:3-4; 107:29.

Chaos and tumult, forces of destruction, surround the disciples in the boat on the stormy sea. This image might refer to the very real waves on the sea or to their strong and diverse opinions that could destroy their discipleship with Jesus. In either case, the raging storm must be calmed or they will be lost. Jesus, who has just come to his own understanding of the power of God within him, now comes to them on the water and uses that power[3] to rescue the disciples. It is in the calming of the waters that the disciples recognize the saving power of Jesus.[4] Impulsive Peter responds to the invitation to walk into this tumult, but he cannot survive it because his faith is plagued with doubt. In a striking parallel to what has just occurred with Jesus in prayer, God's power does not take hold within Peter.

We, too, like Peter, are invited to walk on rough and stormy waters, confident that the power of Jesus will catch us by the hand, embrace, support, and steady us. Elijah discovered this power in the gentle breeze (1 Kgs 19:12); we find it in the midst of the storm, firm in the faith that the power of God alive in Jesus is also alive in us.

---

[3] "Through the sea was your path; / your way, through the mighty waters, / though your footsteps were unseen" (Ps 77:20); "He alone stretches out the heavens / and treads upon the crests of the sea" (Job 9:8).

[4] Jesus shares in the divine power to save. See Psalms 18:17-18; 144:7; Exodus 3:14; Isaiah 43:10; 51:12.

Near the marshy delta where the Jordan meets the northern end of the Sea of Galilee, Bethsaida's fishermen found plentiful catches.

18. Bethsaida

Scripture Reading

Cycle C   The Body and Blood of Christ   Luke 9:11-17

About the Site

Located on the northern edge of the Sea of Galilee, Bethsaida, during the Old Testament period, belonged to the Geshurites and was not part of the kingdom of David and Solomon. King David married a Geshurite princess, and his son by her, Absalom, sought refuge here after killing his half brother Amnon (2 Sam 3:3; 13:38). During the Hellenistic period a new town was built and became one of the largest on the lake.

Bethsaida continued to be a thriving urban center, and after Herod the Great's death, it became part of his son Philip's territory. According to Josephus, Philip favored Bethsaida and had his mausoleum built there, though archaeologists have failed to uncover it.[1] In 30 C.E., Philip granted the town the title of "polis" and renamed it Julias in honor of Livia-Julia, Tiberius's mother. The city was later known as Bethsaida-Julias. During the Jewish Wars the Romans destroyed the city, and it was never substantially reinhabited.

Current excavations have uncovered 150 anchors, lead weights, and needles used in fishing, supporting textual sources that Bethsaida was a center of the fishing industry. The town itself stands on a basalt hill extending from the lower Golan; the buildings and walls uncovered are of roughly hewn basalt stones. Silting from the Jordan and tectonics from the Syro-African rift in which the Jordan valley and the Sea of Galilee are situated have caused a gradual retreating of the lake's shoreline. Once nearer to the Jordan and the Sea of Galilee, today's Tel Bethsaida is one and a quarter miles from the lake.[2]

Reflection

With quiet green eddies, the Jordan River flows south under the planked bridge. A tour bus rumbles over the bridge, disturbing the

[1] Sandra Fortner, University of Munich, Bethsaida Excavation Team tour guide, May 30, 1997.

[2] John J. Rousseau and Rami Arav, *Jesus and His World* (Minneapolis: Fortress, 1995) 21.

birds on the bank and startling a canoeist navigating a bend in the slow river. For a couple of miles the river is more than fifty feet wide before it empties into a marshy delta at the northern end of the Sea of Galilee. Along its course five other streams enter it, depositing various organic material and providing the area in ancient times with some of the best fishing on the Galilee.[3] This location was so noted for its fishing that the settlement which grew up there was named Bethsaida, which in Aramaic means "house of fishing."

The original home of the disciples Peter, Andrew, and Philip (John 1:44), Bethsaida is part of a triad of towns Jesus frequented—Chorazin, Capernaum, and Bethsaida. These three towns are also cursed by Jesus for their unwillingness to repent (Matt 11:21, 23). On a trip to Caesarea Philippi, he encountered a blind man at Bethsaida and healed him (Mark 8:22). To read Luke's account of this Sunday's gospel, the feeding of the five thousand occurred near Bethsaida. The story is found in the other Gospels as well, but the location is south of Capernaum (Mark 6:45; John 6:23) and today is commemorated at Tabgha, at the base of the Mount of Beatitudes.

In what scholars call "The Great Omission," Luke telescopes the Marcan account, eliminating Mark 6:45–8:26. Jesus produces the miracle of the loaves and fishes, and then "once when Jesus was praying in solitude" (Luke 9:18), he asked the disciples who the crowds thought he was. The Marcan stories of walking on water (6:45-52), the healings at Gennesaret (6:43-56), the district of Tyre (7:24-30), the Decapolis (7:31-37), and Bethsaida (8:22-26), and the conversation with the Pharisees (7:1-23) and about the Pharisees (8:14-21) are all omitted. Instead, what Luke has emphasized at the close of Jesus' Galilean ministry is the miracle of the loaves and fishes, the only miracle story to appear in all four Gospels.

Bethsaida in the first century would have been one of the largest cities on the Sea of Galilee. More specifically, its harbor was on the lake, and its principal city buildings were on higher ground above the lake on the east side of the Jordan. At least three of Jesus' disciples were from Bethsaida, the gateway to the tetrarchy of Philip. The presence of good fishing, a tolerant ruler, and the Hellenistic culture creating a "polis" would have made Bethsaida a viable place to live and work.

That Peter and Andrew relocated to Capernaum is clear. Why they did so is speculation. Some have suggested that it was necessary to bring fish to Magdala in the tetrarchy of Herod to be salted. This required crossing a border toll and paying a tax each time, so the move may have been for economic reasons. The illness of Peter's mother-in-

---

[3] Fortner, May 30, 1997.

The ruins of Bethsaida are only recently being excavated.

law in Capernaum may indicate that he relocated for personal reasons (Luke 4:38-39).

While Luke locates his story of the feeding of the five thousand near Bethsaida, the probability of a crowd of that size (larger than most towns and cities at that time) gathering between the ribbon of the Jordan River to its west and the lake to its immediate south is unlikely. The Jordan delta is marshy, and the plain to its east is rocky. In addition, Luke has the Twelve encourage Jesus to dismiss the crowd in order that they might find food and lodging, "for we are in a deserted place here" (9:12). Bethsaida was one of the largest cities on the Sea of Galilee and certainly not "a deserted place."

Today Bethsaida looks down over the Jordan. No longer a harbor for fishers or a thriving Greco-Roman city, the tel at Bethsaida watches as throngs of visitors make their way on its bumpy access road and continue to Jordan Park, where they rent canoes and kayaks. After an outing on the river, the visitors recline in circles under the spray of willows. Pita and fish, grapefruit drink and Cokes fill colorful picnic baskets. Few if any know that on that very site a miracle is remembered.

Looking south along the ancient coast of Phoenicia, one can still see the remnants of rock quarries.

19. The Region of Tyre and Sidon

Scripture Reading

Cycle A	20th Sunday of Ordinary Time	Matt 15:21-28

About the Site

The region of Phoenicia in Jesus' day kept alive the memory of the fierce Sea Peoples who long ago had settled on the coast of Syria-Palestine. The Phoenicians settled the area north of Mount Carmel and, aided by natural harbors, engaged in an extensive sea trade, including the exporting of the cedars of Lebanon that Solomon used in building his Temple.

Geographically, the area is abutted by the Lebanon Mountains from which came the famous "cedars of Lebanon." This highland area extends more than six thousand feet above sea level, with the highest peak being Qurnat el-Sauda at eleven thousand feet above sea level. The central highlands of Palestine are a continuation of this ridge, with the highest point in Upper Galilee. Located about ten miles southwest of Hazor, the peak of Jebel Jermaq is nearly four thousand feet high.[1]

Where the Lebanon Mountains near the coast, a narrow area forms the Plain of Phoenicia. The ability to engage in sea trade enhanced the cosmopolitan nature of its cities, as evidenced in the archaeology of Sidon, Tyre, Gebal, and further north, Ugarit.[2]

The region of Judea in the first century formed the southern boundary of Phoenicia, with the region of Galilee on its eastern edge. Extending north of Caesarea Maritima approximately eighty miles, Phoenicia was primarily a Gentile area of Greeks, Romans, and an indigenous population who even in the first century referred to themselves as Canaanites.[3] At the time of Jesus, it was part of the larger Syrian province under Roman administration.

---

[1] Herbert G. May, "The Fertile Crescent and its Environment," *The Interpreter's One-Volume Commentary on the Bible,* ed. Charles M. Laymon (Nashville: Abingdon, 1971) 1002.

[2] Ibid., 1003.

[3] Howard Clark Kee, "The Gospel According to Matthew," *The Interpreter's One-Volume Commentary on the Bible,* ed. Charles M. Laymon (Nashville: Abingdon, 1971) 628.

Reflection

Matthew mentions the region of Tyre and Sidon on two occasions. First, it is compared to the unrepentant towns Jesus curses: "Woe to you, Chorazin! Woe to you, Bethsaida! For if the mighty deeds done in your midst had been done in Tyre and Sidon, they would long ago have repented in sackcloth and ashes. But I tell you, it will be more tolerable for Tyre and Sidon on the day of judgment than for you" (11:21-22). Indeed, it does go better for one resident of that area (Matt 15). The Canaanite woman stands in sharp contrast to the Pharisees and scribes. In the beginning of chapter 15 she challenges Jesus' purity standards.

Though we have no textual references of Jesus visiting the cities of Tyre or Sidon, we do know that he traveled through the area, perhaps on his way to Caesarea Philippi, north of Galilee. While Matthew's Gospel states that "Jesus went from that place and withdrew to the region of Tyre and Sidon" (Matt 15:21), some biblical scholars assert that it is not Jesus who is in this very pagan area but rather the woman who has come from there to seek Jesus.[4] Wherever they do meet, what ensues is perhaps one of the most unsettling stories about Jesus. A pagan woman (Matthew emphasizes this by changing Mark's "Syrophoenician woman" to "a Canaanite woman") calls out to Jesus, "Lord, Son of David!" an acknowledgment of his status. She implores his help in healing her daughter, only to be rebuked by silence. The silence is broken by her constancy. Finally the disciples implore Jesus, not for the woman's sake, but for their own: "Send her away, for she keeps calling out after us" (Matt 15:23). She pays him homage, according to the text. What follows is Jesus' story of children and dogs, his reassertion in Matthew 10:6 that he has come for the "lost sheep of the house of Israel."

According to Jewish purity laws, Gentiles were outside the bounds of what was considered clean. Proselytes or Gentile converts to Judaism could marry full Israelites and therefore belong to Israel.[5] If this Canaanite is a "God-fearer," she is not so designated. Referring to the woman as a dog is even more troubling. However, in Jewish purity rules animals occupied spheres of cleanliness and uncleanliness similar to those of Israelites and non-Israelites. Hence, dogs belonged to the group of animals excluded from the purity scale.[6] Jesus is reasserting that Gentiles and dogs are both unclean and outside the bounds of his original pastoral vision. Ironically, it would seem that this encounter parallels Jesus' earlier one with the Pharisees and scribes (15:1-20).

[4] John P. Meier, *Matthew* (Wilmington, Del.: Michael Glazier, 1980) 171.

[5] Bruce Malina, *The New Testament World: Insights from Cultural Anthropology* (Louisville, Ky.: Westminster/John Knox, 1993) 160.

[6] Ibid., 164.

While the woman could feel rebuked, she engages in the Mediterranean ethic of honor-shame in such a way as to create a win-win situation. Jesus is obliged by his culture to promote honor, in this case to adhere to his original mission to the lost sheep of Israel. The woman challenges that honor by her very presence. When Jesus explains his situation by the story of children, meals, and dogs, the woman pays him "homage" (v. 25) by promoting positive shame. "Positive shame means sensitivity about one's own reputation, sensitivity to the opinion of others. To have shame in this sense is an eminently positive value."[7] And protecting honor and possessing shame were the responsibilities of women. "Honor as shame or ethical goodness comes from the mother; she symbolizes it."[8] The Canaanite woman recognizes Jesus as "Lord" and "Son of David." She acknowledges his privileged place as a Jew, but at the same time she allows him the opportunity to witness the faith of the "other."

Throughout the Old Testament the Israelites and the Canaanites were at odds. While Israel worshiped Yahweh, the Canaanites worshiped Baʿal and the goddesses of fertility. While the Israelites eked out a living in the highlands as shepherds and farmers, the Canaanites were the more cosmopolitan urban dwellers. Always it seemed that the original inhabitants of Canaan had the upper hand. The one thing Israel had was its tenacious God and its collective consciousness as a chosen people. The Canaanite woman affronts Jesus, and probably more specifically the community of Matthew, with the possibility that those on the outside might be allowed in.

One mile south of the present-day Lebanon-Israel border at Rosh Haniqra, in what long ago was Phoenicia, ancient quarries are visible at the water's edge. Archaeologists have determined that the coastline of kurkar made excellent building stones, but as inland travel was difficult, various peoples cut the stones at the water's edge and then transported the blocks on boats to larger cities. Where the Lebanon Mountains touch the Mediterranean's edge, the cliffs of Rosh Haniqra tower above the quarries. In a time before biblical history, before any history, ancient men and women came to these cliffs, not for the kurkar below, but for a much more valuable stone: flint. Hundreds of thousands of pieces of flint pepper the white limestone wall that falls into the sea. Before the Israelites, before the Phoenicians, before the Canaanites, before people had names and gods and boundaries, the people of the Stone Age chipped their tools from the soft limestone.

[7] Ibid., 50.
[8] Ibid., 53.

While Israeli soldiers patrol the hilltop border, this promontory stands as a sentinel, guarding the edge of hope, remembering when a woman from Lebanon honoring a man from Israel asked for help. And changed them both.

The forum at Gerasa (Jerash) in Jordan evidences the greatest of the cities of the Decapolis.

20. The Area of the Decapolis

Scripture Reading

Cycle B   23rd Sunday of Ordinary Time   Mark 7:31-37

About the Site

The Decapolis, a Greek word meaning "ten cities," refers to a region east of the Sea of Galilee stretching down to the northern edge of the Dead Sea. In Numbers 32:33-42 this area becomes the territory of the tribe of Manasseh. Many Greeks had come to live here in the wake of Alexander's conquests (fourth century B.C.E.). The Romans occupied the area under the leadership of Pompey (65 B.C.E.). It was in this period of Roman strength that the league of ten cities was formed, partially as a source for the influence of Hellenization in the area.[1]

Seven of the cities were located in an area that is present-day Jordan: Abila, Dion, Canatha, Raphana, Jerash, Philadelphia (Amman), and Pella. Three others were within the present borders of Israel. One of these, Gadara (Matt 8:28), is several miles southeast of Kursi (Gergesa) and provides a prime example of Hellenistic culture. The city was built on a hill five miles southeast of the Sea of Galilee. The hot springs (Hammath Gader) found there made it a health spa in the first century. It has been visited for healing ever since. Colonnaded streets, elaborate Roman baths, and the presence of two theaters suggest the amenities of a Greek city.[2] Another, Hippos (Susita in Aramaic), maintained a port on the east side of the Sea of Galilee. Hippos was on the Roman road linking the third city, Scythopolis (Beth Shean), the only city of the Decapolis on the west side of the Jordan River, to Damascus. Damascus, also a city of the Decapolis though not contiguous with the others, was then and is now in Syria.[3] This league of cities had its own coinage, courts, and army. The influence of Greco-Roman culture spilled over from these cities into the neighboring regions

---

[1] Jerome Murphy-O'Connor, O.P., *The Holy Land* (Oxford: Oxford University Press, 1992) 197.

[2] Sherman Johnson, *Jesus and His Towns* (Wilmington, Del.: Michael Glazier, 1989) 78–79.

[3] Raymond Brown, S.S., Joseph Fitzmyer, S.J., Roland Murphy, O Carm., eds., *New Jerome Biblical Commentary* (Englewood Cliffs, N.J.: Prentice Hall, 1990) 588. A map in this commentary locates eleven cities. Another commentary says that there were as many as eighteen. See J. D. Douglas, Merril C. Tenney, *NIV Compact Dictionary of the Bible* (Grand Rapids, Mich.: Zondervan, 1989) 152.

of Galilee and Gaulanitis. For Jews, the area of the Decapolis was Gentile, that is, foreign territory.

Jesus embarks on a journey (Mark 7:24) after a challenging encounter with some Pharisees and other experts in the Law from Jerusalem. The route suggested in the Gospel takes him to the region around Tyre on the coast of the Mediterranean Sea (in present-day Lebanon) and Sidon, which is farther inland. The return itinerary skirts the northern edge of Palestine, possibly through Caesarea Philippi, to the Golan Heights, then south into the area of the Decapolis along the east side of the Sea of Galilee, and eventually back to the west side of the sea at Dalmanutha (Mark 8:10). On the way Jesus has a very significant encounter with a Syro-Phoenician woman (Mark 7:24-30). Jesus was already known in the Decapolis because of the man he freed of his demons at Kursi (Mark 5:1-20). This man was sent "on mission" to the Decapolis (Mark 5:20). The crowds hear of Jesus' presence and bring him their sick to be healed.

Social scientists consider this very long, arduous journey improbable and suggest that the social information in the story might be a more likely source of insight.[4] For example, Jesus travels through territories where his reputation has spread but his family is not known. Not knowing Jesus' origins perhaps removes an obstacle (Matt 13:54-57; Mark 3:20-21) to people's belief in his healing powers. After healing the deaf-mute, there is another great feeding of the multitude (Mark 8:1-20). This feeding takes place among the Gentiles in the Decapolis. Donald Senior, C.P., suggests that the historical fact of the Decapolis as Gentile territory is symbolic as a foreshadowing of the inclusive mission of the post-Easter community.[5]

Reflection

The preceding verses in the Gospel of Mark (7:24-30) provide the setting for the journey that includes the episode recounted in today's gospel reading. It seems that Jesus wanted to be in a place where he was not recognized and could be alone. He believed that Gentile territory would provide a respite from the Pharisees and others who provided a constant challenge to his message (7:24). As often happens when one takes time away from "the job," the change in routine affords an opportunity for new insights and clearer perspectives to come into focus.

---

[4] Bruce Malina and Richard Rohrbaugh, *Social-Science Commentary on the Synoptic Gospels* (Minneapolis: Fortress, 1992) 225.

[5] Donald Senior, C.P., "Decapolis," *Collegeville Dictionary of Pastoral Theology*, ed. Carroll Stuhlmueller (Collegeville, Minn.: The Liturgical Press, 1996) 212–213.

Jesus' conversation with the Syro-Phoenician woman gave him an insight about himself that profoundly affected his ministry. When he refused her request to expel an evil spirit from her daughter on the basis that his mission was to the people of Israel, she did not go away quietly. Her rebuttal that "even the dogs under the table eat the children's scraps" (Mark 7:28) startled him. Jesus had taught others that religious customs should not be a barrier to helping someone in need (see Mark 2:23-28; 3:1-6).[6] This woman's words may have challenged Jesus in the same way he had challenged the Pharisees. From this moment his perspective on his own mission changed from one of exclusivity to one of inclusivity. His purpose while he was in the region of Tyre and Sidon (later continuing into the area of the Decapolis, where today's reading takes place) changed from a time of escape, not being recognized, to an expansion of his ministry beyond the Jews.

When Jesus reached the area of the Decapolis, his reputation preceded him. The people there were ready and eager to listen to him. He did not disappoint them. A deaf man with a speech impediment was brought to him. Jesus took him to a place of privacy to perform a healing ritual. His actions, for example spitting and the use of certain words, were typical of traditional healers.[7] It was assumed that illness was the result of an evil spirit. Spitting was one of several practices believed to ward off evil. The words spoken in a healing ritual were believed to have power embedded in them. So the Gospel writer includes "Ephphatha!" in its original Aramaic when telling the story.

Even though the healing took place in private, the results were soon public. The crowds were amazed at Jesus' power. Despite his request not to tell anyone, the crowds began to proclaim what they had seen: "He has done all things well! He makes the deaf hear and [the] mute speak!" (Mark 7:37). The use of the verb "proclaim" to describe the action of the crowd is significant. They recognized that Jesus was more than a healer. Throughout the Gospel of Mark, it is the gospel, the good news of salvation through Jesus, that is *proclaimed* (see 1:14; 13:10; 14:9). The Gentiles in the area of the Decapolis recognized and proclaimed the saving power of Jesus. Their words echo Isaiah's proclamation of Israel's deliverance from exile:

> Then will the eyes of the blind be opened,
>   the ears of the deaf be cleared;
> Then will the lame leap like a stag,
>   then the tongue of the dumb will sing (Isa 35:5-6).

---

[6] Carol Newsom and Sharon Ringe, eds., *The Women's Bible Commentary* (Louisville, Ky.: Westminster/John Knox, 1992) 269.

[7] Malina and Rohrbaugh, *Social-Science Commentary on the Synoptic Gospels*, 225.

Jesus, who went into Gentile territory because he didn't want to be recognized by others, instead comes to a new recognition of his mission, which in turn enables others to recognize in him the liberating power of God.

We hear strange things in the gospel: we must die in order to live, be blind so as to see, deaf so that we can hear, be last to be first, lose to gain. These enigmatic statements suggest a way of life and a set of values quite opposite to those of our society. St. Paul tells the Colossians:

> Think of what is above, not of what is on earth. For you have died, and your life is hidden with Christ in God. When Christ your life appears, then you too will appear with him in glory (Col 3:2-4).

Our own transformation in grace will come when we recognize that the living risen Christ is our salvation. This new life in Christ is God's gift.

The caves of Pan are niches in the rock face where statues once stood.

21. Caesarea Philippi

Scripture Readings

Cycle A	21st Sunday of Ordinary Time	Matt 16:13-20
	22nd Sunday of Ordinary Time	Matt 16:21-27
Cycle B	24th Sunday of Ordinary Time	Mark 8:27-35

About the Site

A fault line from Acco, on the Mediterranean coast, running past the north end of the Sea of Galilee separates the region into Upper and Lower Galilee. The terrain of these two areas differs significantly. Upper Galilee is dominated by rugged mountains. Mount Habetarim and Mount Dor are part of the Hermon Range north and east of the sea. Mount Hermon is the highest peak of the range at 6,670 feet and is snow-covered through much of the year. Villages in this mountainous area have always remained relatively isolated not only from the other regions of Galilee but from one another as well. This remoteness and isolation allowed the area to become "a haven from political and religious persecution, an environment for hermits, bandits and colonies of purist religious observance."[1]

The headwaters of the Jordan are in these mountains. The river carries this fresh water to the Sea of Galilee. In the first century one could navigate from the sea up the Jordan River about a mile to the village of Bethsaida, the home of Andrew (John 12:21) and perhaps other apostles. From there it was a long day's journey on foot to the base of the southern slope of Mount Hermon to a place called Panias. The rugged travel is worth the reward. Panias, named after the god Pan, is lush with vegetation and filled with the sound of running brooks. At the base of a limestone cliff is a large cave. Though the mouth of the cave is now covered by fallen rocks due to an earthquake, streams of water flowing from beneath the rocks form the beginning of the Jordan River. The beauty of this place made it a sanctuary from earliest times. Niches in the face of the cliff held statues of the god Pan, a perfect setting for a nature god. Josephus describes the area and a temple that Herod the Great built there in honor of Augustus:

---

[1] Anne Hennessy, C.S.J., *The Galilee of Jesus* (Rome: Editrice Pontificia Universita Gregoriana, 1994) 9.

> There is a very fine cave in a mountain under which there is a great cavity in the earth, and the cavern is abrupt and prodigiously deep and full of still water; over it hangs a vast mountain, and under the caverns arise the springs of the Jordan. Herod adorned this place, which was already a very remarkable one, still further by the erection of this temple, which he dedicated to Caesar.[2]

After Herod's death Panias passed to his son Philip, who made it the capital of his territory and named it Caesarea Philippi in honor of Caesar Augustus and himself. Visitors in the first century, such as Jesus and his disciples, or those who were permanent residents would have lived in the midst of natural beauty and great wealth, extensive public buildings, temples and pagan gods. The military power of Rome was very evident.

As for the political climate of the area, among the Jews, the Pharisees and Zealots were hoping for a messiah who would lead them in the struggle against Rome. The Zealots, as their name suggests, were more aggressive, even violent, in this struggle. The Zealot party was founded in 6 c.e. in the city of Gamla, near Bethsaida to the east. Jews from Bethsaida would certainly have had personal contact with members of the Zealot party. Indeed, one of the apostles was named Simon the Zealot. The Herodian dynasty (Herod Antipas, tetrarch of Galilee and his brother Herod Philip, tetrarch of Gaulanitis) were loyal to Rome.

Jesus took his closest disciples to an area named for Caesar, with a temple to Caesar, surrounded by pagan idolatry, but also a place of strong and majestic mountains, fertile soil, beautiful trees and flowers, and the source of fresh, clear water to have a serious talk with them about the concept of Messiah. The parallels are striking: that which is brought about by human hand, military power, and worldly wealth is a way of leadership that leads to domination; the life and strength and beauty provided by the gracious gift of God is a way of living that leads to freedom.

Today the city with its temples is gone but the beauty remains. The area is a national park, with the cave of Pan still the centerpiece. It is called Banias, a corruption of Panias.

Reflection

From the time of the destruction of the first Jerusalem Temple in 587 B.C.E., the Jewish people believed that one day a leader would ap-

---

[2] Josephus, *Antiquities*, XV, 10, 3.

pear who would restore their identity as a people. Concepts of king, prophet, and military leader were intertwined in various descriptions of who this person would be and what he would do.[3] One commonality in these references was the title given him: Messiah, meaning "the anointed one."

The political climate for the Jews in the early first century was one of desperation. The overpowering Roman Empire was usurping even the slight vestige of leadership they had left. Every Jewish mother hoped that she would be the one who would give birth to the Messiah. Every Jewish boy wondered at some moment in his life if he might be the anointed one. The small band of followers who accompanied Jesus to Caesarea Philippi knew that this itinerant preacher to whom they were devoted was someone very significant; however, they were not prepared for the revelation that was about to take place. When Jesus posed the question "Who do people say that the Son of Man is?" (Matt 16:13; Mark 8:27), he did not know the answer himself. This was not a test to see if the disciples understood him and his mission. Mediterranean culture in the first century (and to some extent today) was dyadic, that is, other-centered.[4] Family origins and behavior that were considered honorable or shameful governed one's place in society. One's identity came from what other significant people thought of you, not what you thought of yourself. Position and power resulted from honor status, not from personal identity.

The disciples' response gave Jesus important information: "Some say John the Baptist, others Elijah, still others Jeremiah or one of the prophets" (Matt 16:14; Mark 8:28). Herod thought that Jesus was John the Baptist raised from the dead, because "mighty powers are at work in him"(Matt 14:2). Elijah was taken heavenward in a fiery chariot (2 Kgs 2:11). It was Jewish tradition that he would return from heaven to prepare Israel for the final manifestation of God's kingdom.[5] Jeremiah the prophet suffered arrest, imprisonment, and public disgrace. While

---

[3] Leslie Hoppe, O.F.M., "Messiah," *The Collegeville Dictionary of Biblical Theology*, ed. Carroll Stuhlmueller, C.P. (Collegeville, Minn.: The Liturgical Press, 1996) 615–620.

[4] Malina and Rohrbaugh, *Social-Science Commentary on the Synoptic Gospels* (Minneapolis: Fortress, 1992) 113.

[5] The source for this tradition is Malachi 3:23-24:

> Lo, I will send you
>> Elijah, the prophet,
> Before the day of the LORD comes.
>> the great and terrible day,
> To turn the hearts of the fathers to their children,
>> and the hearts of the children to their fathers.

experiencing his own rejection, he announced the rejection of the Messiah. It was Jeremiah who announced a new covenant.[6]

Like a puzzle with the pieces falling into place, each of these names —John the Baptist, Elijah, Jeremiah—would give Jesus a little clearer picture of who he was. The response to Jesus' next question, "But who do you say that I am?" snapped the picture into focus. "You are the Messiah, the Son of the living God."

This profound moment was a turning point in the life of Jesus. To mark the significant role of Peter in this event and the future of this community, his name was changed. Cephas became Peter ("rock"). His witness to Jesus as Messiah became the foundation of faith for us, the post-resurrection community.

What follows immediately in the next verses of the Gospel are consequences of this focusing of Jesus' identity. Previously Jesus responded to queries about his character with a command of silence. Now he is bold. He predicts his own suffering and death, and firmly rebukes Peter's lack of understanding. It is not only his own life that is clear now; what it means to be a follower of Jesus is given clarity too. The conditions of discipleship are announced: Deny yourself, take up your cross, lose your life in order to save it, forfeit the world and gain your life. All the expectations surrounding the Messiah in Jewish tradition are turned upside down.

The question is posed to each of us, too. "Who do you say that I am?" A response like Peter's would give focus and meaning to our lives—and perhaps turn us upside down.

[6]Jer 31:31-34.

In Jordan, Mount Nebo is the site that commemorates Moses' looking into the Promised Land. Here on the east side of the Jordan River Valley, the first-century pilgrims from Galilee would often travel to avoid Samaria.

22. The District of Judea, Across the Jordan

Scripture Readings

Cycle A	25th Sunday of Ordinary Time	Matt 20:1-16
Cycle B	27–29th Sundays of Ordinary Time	Mark 10:2-43

About the Site

The Syro-African rift begins north of Israel/Palestine. Its eastern boundary is the Jordan River; turning slightly westward, the rift is called Arabah, south of the Dead Sea. Reaching water, it forms the Gulf of Aqabah, continuing through the Red Sea and into Africa. The Jordan River meanders for sixty-five miles through this valley, falling from 675 feet below sea level at the Sea of Galilee to 1,300 feet below at the Dead Sea. Nearly twenty miles wide in sections, the valley is rimmed with mountains rising one thousand feet or more. The Arabic word for the valley is "Ghor."

Within this valley is a second, narrower valley cut by the descending Jordan. The "Zor," or "thicket," as this second valley is called, is one mile wide and nearly 150 feet lower than the Ghor. Here the river is only sixty to eighty feet wide.[1] Rising up from the Zor are ash-gray marl hills with barren, crumbly soil called "qattara." Uncultivated, this area was once known for its wild animals—lions (Jer 49:19; 50:44; Zech 11:3), tigers, wild boar, jackals, desert rats, otters, and, as recently as 1898, bears. Jordan tamarisk, willow, the Euphrates poplar, oleander, reeds, thorns, and thistles continue to grow along the narrow ribbon of the Jordan.[2]

As the Jordan River descends, it is joined by fourteen major and secondary wadis along its route to the Dead Sea. The largest tributaries to the Jordan are the Yarmuk and the Jabbok Rivers. Nine other wadis flow from the east. Because of the presence of a consistent water supply, the eastern side was always more inhabited. The mountains of either side help keep temperatures mild during winter. The mean summer temperature is about 87 degrees, with extreme temperatures

---

[1] Raymond E. Brown, S.S., and Robert North, S.J., "Biblical Geography," *The New Jerome Biblical Commentary* (Englewood Cliffs, N.J.: Prentice Hall, 1990) 1185.

[2] Henry O. Thompson, "Jordan, jungle of," *Anchor Bible Dictionary*, ed. David Freedman (New York: Doubleday, 1992) 3:961.

reaching 106 degrees. The average winter temperature is 58 degrees, with occasional dips into the 40s.[3]

In the first century, Roman roads provided swift travel between major cities. One north-south route through the valley came from Caesarea Philippi, probably along the east bank of the Jordan and the Sea of Galilee to Scythopolis (Beth Shean). At Scythopolis travelers could take a route west to Neapolis (Samaria) or south to Jerusalem via Jericho.[4]

Reflection

According to the Torah, every Jewish man was to make a pilgrimage to Jerusalem.

> Three times a year, then, every male among you shall appear before the LORD, your God, in the place which he chooses [Jerusalem]: at the feast of Unleavened Bread, at the feast of Weeks, and at the feast of Booths. No one shall appear before the LORD empty-handed, but each of you with as much as he can give, in proportion to the blessings which the LORD, your God, has bestowed on you (Deut 16:16-17).

Far from being a religious burden, "pilgrimage to Jerusalem was a communal undertaking, a joyous and happy occasion as people from the same town or village traveled to the holy city in the company of fellow Jews. The historian Josephus said pilgrimage fostered 'mutual affection among Jews.'"[5]

As Jesus left the area of Galilee, he traveled "to the district of Judea across the Jordan" (Matt 19:1), "going up to Jerusalem (Matt 20:17). He and the disciples chose the pilgrimage route that traversed the Jordan rather than the quicker route through Samaria. His last pilgrimage to Jerusalem would be a continuation of his ministry in Galilee. He continued to teach and bless, challenge and heal. Along the way, he announced his third prediction of the Passion and then admonished that leaders in his community must first be servants: "Whoever wishes to be great among you shall be your servant" (Matt 20:26).

---

[3] M. Ibrahim, "Jordan Valley," *Anchor Bible Dictionary,* ed. David Freedman (New York: Doubleday, 1992) 3:958.

[4] David F. Graf, "Roman Roads," *Anchor Bible Dictionary,* ed. David Freedman (New York: Doubleday, 1992) 5:783.

[5] Robert L. Wilken, *The Land Called Holy* (New Haven, Conn.: Yale University Press, 1992) 105.

As Jesus moved closer to Jerusalem, he passed through heavily Gentile territory. The east side of the Sea of Galilee was known as the area of the Decapolis. He would have passed Bethsaida, then Hippos, perched above the sea on a steep hill. Farther south was Gadara, near the place where he cast the demons into the swine. These cities sported monumental buildings and columned streets. Hellenized Jews were among the population. At the southern end of the Sea of Galilee, the road crossed the Jordan to its western bank and continued to Scythopolis. The first leg of the journey was through Greco-Roman cities, along the familiar coast of the lake.

Pilgrimage is an act of worship, of purification, of offering sacrifice. The journey was part of the preparation. Traveling in the spring, Jesus and the disciples would have been surrounded by the beauty of the Jordan Valley, alive with color. Whether Jesus knew what awaited him in Jerusalem, he certainly sensed the growing hostility. Perhaps Jesus chose this longer route of pilgrimage because it afforded him a little longer time to relish his community, to revel in the excitement of the journey, and to ready himself for what lay ahead.

From the ancient tel at Jericho, the Mount of Temptation rises in the background.

23. Jericho

Scripture Readings

| Cycle B | 30th Sunday of Ordinary Time | Mark 10:46-53 |
| Cycle C | 31st Sunday of Ordinary Time | Luke 19:1-10 |

About the Site

Tel es-Sultan, Old Testament Jericho, is the oldest city on earth. Archaeologists date its earliest settlement at 8,000 B.C.E. By 7,000 B.C.E., "the city was enclosed in a strong stone wall, with one of its towers still standing to a height of 7.75 meters."[1] Jericho is also the lowest city on earth, 770 feet below sea level, a tremendous drop from Jerusalem, just twenty-three miles east and 2,500 feet above sea level.

Though couched at the foot of the Judean desert and the Jordan rift valley, Jericho is an oasis, thanks to the Fountain of Elisha, which pours forth a thousand gallons of water a minute. The Book of Joshua recounts a vivid tale of the capture of Jericho, but archaeological evidence shows that no large walled city existed at the time. Further, biblical scholars note that the story of the fall of Jericho belongs to a later editor, probably the Priestly source. A band of prophets was located here in the time of Elijah, who met with them shortly before his departure. His protégé, Elisha, purified the springs after his master's disappearance in a whirlwind on the other side of the Jordan.

As an oasis, the area is filled with lush vegetation. The date palms and persimmons were highly prized in antiquity. The perfume from the persimmon was so sought after that Mark Antony gave an estate at the edge of the Dead Sea to Cleopatra (34 B.C.E.), who later leased it to Herod the Great.[2]

Archaeology of New Testament Jericho showed that Hasmonean and Herodian palaces were located at the upper part of the oasis, close to the eastern edges of the hills, near the location where the ancient road led to Jerusalem.[3] Herod the Great received the palace and estate after the battle of Actium, but an earthquake in 31 B.C.E. necessitated its

---

[1] Jack Finegan, *The Archaeology of the New Testament* (Princeton, N.J.: Princeton University Press, 1992) 145.

[2] John J. Rousseau and Rami Arav, *Jesus and His World* (Minneapolis: Fortress, 1995) 132.

[3] Ibid., 133.

rebuilding. The resulting edifice eclipsed the early Hasmonean structures in size and opulence. Herod utilized the best of Roman architecture in his elaborate building campaign at Jericho. It was in this palace
that Herod died.[4]

Jericho, because of its temperate climate in winter, became the
haven for Jerusalem's elite. Archaeology uncovered extravagant buildings, pools, and gardens. A luxuriant oasis, Jericho was also heavily
protected by Roman detachments lodged in the nearby hills. The
arable plain, abundance of water, and proximity to trade routes made
first-century Jericho a wealthy city. In addition to its date palms, bal-
sam, cypress, and myrobalanus, sycamore trees grew in and around
New Testament Jericho. Timber from the sycamore was found in a Hellenistic fort near the area. Today a sycamore graces the central square
in modern Jericho.

Reflection

The pilgrimage route from Galilee and the Decapolis came up from
Jericho, climbing more than 3,200 feet from below sea level. The Romans paved the road and set mile markers at various points. The road
followed the Wadi Qelt for more than three miles and then probably
went southwest. Along the route there are visible ruins of bridges and
aqueducts that brought water from the three large springs in the wadi
to the pools and palaces in New Testament Jericho. About five miles
west of Jericho, the Roman road went through a pass that is 885 feet
above sea level and 1,655 feet above Jericho.[5] The modern road follows
the Roman road through this pass today. The Arabic name for the pass
is *tal'at eddamm,* meaning "ascent of blood," which corresponds to the
Hebrew for "ascent of adummim," probably referring not to blood but
to the red marl of the pass. This area came to be known as the site of
the Good Samaritan. Crusader Burchard of Mount Sion wrote of this
area:

> Four leagues to the west of Jericho, on the road to Jerusalem, to the
> left of Quarentena, is the Castle of Adummim, the place where the
> man who went down from Jerusalem to Jericho fell among
> thieves. This has befallen many on the same spot in modern times,
> and the place has received its name from the frequent blood shed
> there. Of a truth it is horrible to behold, and exceeding dangerous,
> unless one travels with an escort.[6]

[4] Finegan, *The Archaeology of the New Testament,* 148.
[5] Ibid., 153.
[6] Ibid., 154.

The modern city of Jericho continues to thrive on the water from the En es-Sultan spring.

While Jesus' parable of the Good Samaritan is a story designed to answer the question "Who is my neighbor?" certainly the route to Jerusalem was dangerous. Even the Gospels indicate that Jesus was with his disciples and a "sizable crowd" (Mark 10:46). Traveling en masse was certainly safer, but the "crowd" may also indicate a period of pilgrimage. Three times during the year, Jews were required to make a pilgrimage to Jerusalem: the feast of Tabernacles in the fall, the feast of Passover in the spring, and the feast of Shavuot (Pentecost) in the summer. Excavations south of the Temple area in Jerusalem indicate ritual baths designed for pilgrim use prior to entering the city.[7]

Two Sunday gospels are located in Jericho; one concerns a wealthy cheat and another tells of a blind man. One presents the wealthy of Jericho, the ones living in the fine homes. The other is about a beggar clinging to the outskirts of the city, hoping that the pilgrims will be generous. Both desire to see. Both are changed by their encounter with Jesus.

Today the steep climb up from Jericho reminds one that pilgrimages were always difficult, that a faith-response is never an easy path. As even the newest vehicles inch their way up the asphalt out of the

[7] Leslie J. Hoppe, O.F.M., "Pilgrimage," *The Collegeville Pastoral Dictionary*, ed. Carroll Stuhlmueller (Collegeville, Minn.: The Liturgical Press, 1996) 737.

Jordan Valley, Bedouin tents become visible in narrow canyons. Shepherds herd black goats over the rough hillsides. Then suddenly, as if a
mirage, a staggeringly large settlement appears on a high bluff. Awk-
wardly out of place in this wilderness of shepherds and sheep, Maʾale
Adummim is a sprawling Jewish settlement on the West Bank. What
in 1994 was only a few lights visible from el Azariyeh (Bethany),
Maʾale Adummim holds hundreds of homes now, encircled by walls
and fences and armed guards. Where rough roads led the adventuresome down to the Dead Sea, now a new paved road splits off from the
Jericho road, pausing at the guardhouse before continuing up the
heights to the settlement. The Hebrew "adummim" may mean "red"
and refer to the rocks at the pass, but to the Arabs it is "blood," a flag
waved in the face of the peace process.

It is easy to see in the West Bank settlers the wealthy face of Zac-
chaeus. Easier still to see is the blind beggar Bartimaeus in the eyes of
anguished Arabs. Both are in need of sight. The arduous pilgrimage to
peace in the Holy Land passes through these two blind extremes. May
Jesus, the Son of David and a Prophet of Islam, grant sight to both.

This model at the Holy Land Hotel in Jerusalem shows the Temple as it existed in 66 C.E. It is made on a 1:50 scale.

24. The Temple Area

Scripture Readings

Cycle A	26–31st Sundays of Ordinary Time	Matt 21:28–23:12
	4th Sunday of Easter	John 10:1-10
Cycle B	Holy Family	Luke 2:22-40
	3rd Sunday of Lent	John 2:13-25
	5th Sunday of Lent	John 12:20-33
	4th Sunday of Easter	John 10:11-18
	31–32nd Sundays of Ordinary Time	Mark 12:28-34, 38-44
Cycle C	1st Sunday of Advent	Luke 21:25-28, 34-36
	Holy Family	Luke 2:41-52
	5th Sunday of Lent	John 8:1-11
	4th Sunday of Easter	John 10:27-30
	32nd Sunday of Ordinary Time	Luke 20:27-38
	33rd Sunday of Ordinary Time	Luke 21:5-19

About the Site

When Israelite pilgrims crested the Mount of Olives on their so-journ up to Jerusalem, they were greeted by a massive white limestone Temple glimmering gold in the morning light. The Temple area measured 1,041 feet on the north, 1,556 feet on the east, 929 feet on the south, and 1,596 feet on the west.[1] The size of the platform was roughly five football fields in length and three in width. But the Temple in the first century was actually the third Temple to stand on the site, which was originally the threshing floor of Araunah the Jebusite, which David purchased in order to build an altar (2 Sam 24:18). The site was also known as Mount Moriah, where Abraham attempted to sacrifice his son Isaac.

King Solomon began a massive building campaign in 957 B.C.E., utilizing Phoenician architects, cedars from Lebanon, and thousands of impressed laborers. This Temple housing the ark of the covenant would be God's dwelling on earth.

> This word of the LORD came to Solomon: "As to this temple you are building—if you observe my statutes, carry out my ordinances, keep and obey all my commands, I will fulfill toward you the promise I made to your father David. I will dwell in the midst of the Israelites and will not forsake my people Israel" (1 Kgs 6:11-13).

[1] John J. Rousseau and Rami Arav, *Jesus and His World* (Minneapolis: Fortress, 1995) 280.

149

The Temple was destroyed during the Babylonian siege of 587 B.C.E. The Second Temple was rededicated in 515 B.C.E. having been built by the exiles who had returned from Babylon.

In 20–19 B.C.E., Herod the Great, in an attempt to gain favor with the Jews, enlarged and renovated the Temple. He succeeded in building the largest holy structure in the Greco-Roman world. The Temple esplanade of Herod extended to twice its original size. This required extensive building of retaining walls. Even these less visible structures were decorated with dressed ashlars, the remnants of which are seen at the Western Wall today.

The largest area of the Temple precincts was the Court of the Gentiles, which was open to all. Lining this court were various colonnades and porticos, one of which was called Solomon's Portico, possibly because it included part of the walls dating from the First Temple. Solomon's Portico probably was the eastern colonnade, six hundred feet in length. With a width of forty-five feet and a height of thirty-seven feet, these double colonnades along the sides of the Temple platform provided shelter for the throngs, particularly during pilgrim festivals. The colonnade on the southern side was called the Royal Stoa, a vast basilica-like area where rabbis would teach and merchants would sell the necessary animals for sacrifice. Money changers would also have gathered in this area. Two huge stairs led people through the southern Hulda Gates up to the Temple platform and emerged at the Royal Stoa.

The sacred center of the Temple had areas reserved for the Israelites alone. The first opening was lined by a stone lattice or balustrade bearing warnings for Gentiles not to enter. In 1871 and in 1935, archaeologists uncovered such warning slabs with Greek inscriptions reading "No Gentiles should go beyond this sign under penalty of death."[2] Up fourteen steps was the Court of Women (202 feet square), with the Chamber of the Nazirites in the southeast part, the Chamber of Oil in the southwest, the Chamber of the Lepers in the northwest, and the Chamber of Wood in the northeast.[3] Probably in this area were "shofarot," or treasury boxes, into which the widow of Luke 21:1-4 would have placed her small coins.

Fifteen steps led from the Court of Women to the Court of Israel, where only men could enter. In the passageway stood a 172-foot-high embossed bronzed door. "All the other gates of the sanctuary were plated with silver and gold."[4] The Court of Israel was 202 feet wide but

[2] Ibid., 313.
[3] Ibid., 282.
[4] Ibid.

A young man celebrates his bar mitzvah at the Western Wall.

only seventeen feet deep and stood directly in front of the Court of the Priests. A wall sixty-six feet high surrounded the inner courts of the sanctuary; on it hung spoils taken by the Hasmoneans and Herod the Great. On certain occasions non-priests could go into the Court of the Priests. Within the Court of the Priests, which measured 290 feet by 202 feet, were twenty-four rings for tying animals for sacrifice, an altar for burnt offerings, and a place for the priests to wash their hands and feet. "Marble pillars supported cedar beams on which the carcasses were hooked for skinning."[5]

The sanctuary itself was sixty feet by thirty feet, with walls of plated gold. The altar of incense, the table of the bread of the presence, the golden menorah, and other necessary instruments were located here. Behind a double curtain was a thirty-foot square known as the Holy of Holies. It stood empty in the first century, having once held the ark of the covenant, which disappeared probably during the Babylonian assault. It was here that the Divine touched the earth, and a priest entered this space only once a year on the Day of Atonement.[6]

[5] Ibid.
[6] Ibid., 285.

Reflection

For a people under Roman rule, the center of cultic activities served as the single most important site for all Israel. The rulers of Israel may have had little to say about their political situation, but they had great influence over its religion. Even its political parties were aligned according to their interpretation of the Law. The Pharisees believed in the oral interpretation of Moses and the teaching on resurrection, while the Sadducees held only the Torah was authoritative and did not believe in resurrection. The Sadducees located power in the Temple and its priests, while the Pharisees preferred the local synagogues and rabbis. It would be a mistake to read the Gospels as if Jesus were anti-Jewish. He was, like most in his age, concerned with the life of Israel and most often agreed with Pharisaical tenets. Any anti-Semitic statements are more likely the view of the community that wrote the Gospels, having recently been ousted from the synagogues.

While Jesus' parables and beatitudes give a clear indication of his concern for the poor, the little ones, the sick, and those on the margins of society, his teachings concerning the Temple perhaps provoked the religious authorities the most. In one moment the Gospel writer retells a poignant story of a widow offering all she has to sustain her religion; in the next moment people are praising the "costly stones and votive offerings" (Luke 21:5) that adorn the Temple. "All that you see here— the days will come when there will not be left a stone upon another stone that will not be thrown down," Jesus responds.

Like John the Baptist before him, Jesus preaches a purification of faith, a repentance of sin, a return to the spirit of the Torah and not the letter of the Law. The Temple represents for Jesus the enshrinement of religiosity and not a house of prayer. According to the Synoptics, Jesus' cleansing of the Temple occurred on his last visit to Jerusalem. It was this act that provoked the chief priests and scribes to seek "a way to put him to death" (Mark 11:18). John places this occurrence early in Jesus' ministry.

As Jesus climbed the steep Mount of Olives on his way to the Holy City and its tremendous Temple, he was profoundly moved. "As he drew near, he saw the city and wept over it, saying, 'If this day you only knew what makes for peace—but now it is hidden from your eyes'" (Luke 19:41). Approaching the city today from Bethany is best done on foot. The hike up the narrow road past Bethphage allows the stalwart pilgrim a chance to feel what thousands of pilgrims have felt before—the rush of the holy. After cresting the hill and inching past the tour buses at Pater Noster, the Old City comes into view. Clutching onto the edge of the Kidron Valley is the Temple platform. More than

The Western Wall, where Jews come to pray, is the last remnant of the Second Temple. A fence divides the men's area from the women's.

two thousand years after Herod the Great's expansive remodeling, the ancient stones still glimmer in the afternoon sun.

But even more brilliant than the huge Herodian stones is the Golden Dome of the Rock. This octagonal structure is built over the rock that Muslims believed Mohammed touched on one of his night journeys. That same rock is believed to be Mount Moriah, where Abraham prepared to sacrifice Isaac. Sacred also to the Jews, it may be where the Holy of Holies was located. To see the massive Temple platform, with its radiant mosque encircled in sixteenth-century stone walls, is to see into history. Most Christian pilgrims satisfy themselves with the stories of Jesus and the Temple, failing to appreciate its vast history.

What makes a site holy? Perhaps it is simply the fervent prayers of the faithful, longing for their God. While the Temple platform is crowded with Muslims at prayer on a Friday afternoon, Jews are gathering at the Western Wall, one of the retaining walls of Herod the Great. They will await the call of the shofar and the beginning of Sabbath. When the horn blows, young men in black pants and white shirts will dance arm in arm from the nearby yeshiva. They will sing the prayers of old, while nearby some young boy will be bar mitzvahed. The Christian presence is only a few blocks away. The bells of the Holy Sepulcher ring as pilgrims weary from the weight of their rented crosses finish the Stations of the Cross on the Via Dolorosa.

The most amazing confluence of religion and religiousness, the Temple remains today a symbol of both hope and despair. The Muslims fear that the Jews will take away their right to worship there. Some Jews want to rebuild the Temple. Palestinian Christians from places like Bethlehem cannot even visit. And the words of Jesus echo painfully:

> Jerusalem, Jerusalem, you who kill the prophets and stone those sent to you, how many times I yearned to gather your children together, as a hen gathers her young under her wings, but you were unwilling (Matt 23:37).

Rising out of a field of sunflowers, Mount Tabor continues to create a feeling of awe and mystery.

25. Mount Tabor

Scripture Readings

Cycle A	2nd Sunday of Lent	Matt 17:1-9
Cycle B	2nd Sunday of Lent	Mark 9:2-10
Cycle C	2nd Sunday of Lent	Luke 9:28-36

About the Site

From the 1800-foot summit of Mount Tabor, one has a commanding view. North, in the far distance, is Mount Hermon, the other site once considered the location of the transfiguration. In the foreground are the Horns of Hittim, and a little beyond, a glimpse of the Sea of Galilee. To the west the city of Nazareth is visible, its suburbs spreading down its hills. The mountains of Samaria in the northwest and the range of Carmel in the southwest form the borders of the Jezreel Valley, spreading out at the base of Mount Tabor. In the east, as far away as ancient Hippos, in the area of the Decapolis, Mount Tabor can be seen, its conical plateau towering above the Lower Galilee.

Biblical references suggest that Mount Tabor was a site of Israelite religious worship (Deut 33:18-19; Hos 5:1). Also, it may have been a holy site for the Canaanites even earlier. The nexus for the three tribes of Zebulun, Issachar, and Naphtali, Mount Tabor served as the gathering spot for the tribes in the battle of Deborah (Judg 4:6, 12, 14). When nine hundred Canaanite chariots from Hazor began to attack the Israelite tribes, an unexpected rain clogged their wheels, allowing an Israelite victory.

Though no water source exists on the summit, some habitation did occur there—an Egyptian garrison was quartered on its plateau in the third century B.C.E. In the first century, Josephus himself unsuccessfully fortified Mount Tabor against the Romans. It was later captured in 67.[1]

Though none of the Gospel accounts name Mount Tabor, the story of the transfiguration was situated there by the fourth century. Earlier Eusebius had suggested either Mount Tabor or Mount Hermon, which was located in the tetrarchy of Herod Philip. Some scholars suggest

---

[1] Jerome Murphy-O'Connor, O.P., *The Holy Land* (New York: Oxford University Press, 1992) 369.

that Mount Hermon is the more likely of the two, since Mount Tabor was located in the region of Herod Antipas, who was openly hostile to Jesus. The Pilgrim of Bordeaux (333) locates the transfiguration on the Mount of Olives. Jerome, Cyril of Jerusalem, and Epiphanius all support Mount Tabor.

By the end of the fifth century, mention is made of religious structures on the site. The buildings may have stood until their destruction in the twelfth century by a Turkish attack. In 1924 the Franciscans built a church with splendid mosaics of Jesus, Elijah, and Moses in its sanctuary. The Franciscan church is built upon the Crusader and Byzantine ruins. Today the summit is divided between the Franciscans and the Greek Orthodox. With the hill's steep sides and narrow roadway, tour buses are unable to navigate the curves. Visitors must take a harrowing ride in a local taxi up the mountainside. After such a ride, the passenger may, like Jesus, appear "white, such as no fuller on earth could bleach" (Mark 9:3).

Reflection

The story of the transfiguration is a pivotal moment, a moment that affirmed for Jesus that all he would be about was worth it. On the north side of the mountain is where his ministry in Galilee took place, where he has announced the Good News, gathered disciples, and healed the sick. On the south side was his journey to Jerusalem, where, according to his predictions, he would die. The experience commemorated on Mount Tabor is most often seen as an experience of Jesus' divinity, but the Jesus encountered on the mountain is very human. This Jesus has a choice to make.

Jesus climbed the mountain to pray, and his prayer was so intense it became visible. And behold, two people were conversing with him. What was the conversation among the three? They were talking about the exodus Jesus would fulfill in Jerusalem. The word "exodus" brings memories of Moses and the Israelites escaping from Egypt, God's original salvific act for the chosen people, a salvific act begun with an experience of God on another mountain. As Jesus was filled with an interior assurance, as his face glowed with a new realization, he came to see his ascent to Jerusalem as a saving action. He may, indeed, die in Jerusalem, but that will not be the final word. His death will be an exodus for his people. The reign of God will not be nailed to the wood. The echoes of good news and healing and love and forgiveness will not fade on Calvary. That's what dawned upon the face of Jesus. All will not be lost. Passion, crucifixion, death are but part. Resurrection is the final word. And that word belongs to God.

The power of that insight awakened the three disciples, and as was characteristic of the disciples, they did not get it. Peter put his foot in his mouth. Luke says, "He did not know what he was saying" (9:33). But, maybe he did. Maybe Peter experienced the glory of God and said, "Let's put up camp. Let's stay on the mountain." Peter may have been impetuous, but he was not dumb. He remembered Jesus' admonition that anyone who loses his life will save it. That the follower of Jesus must carry his cross. That Jesus himself will be killed. Knowing all that, why would one leave the mountain?

But the purpose of the transfiguration was not to camp. It was to carry on. The voice of God echoed from the cloud, "This is my chosen Son; listen to him" (Luke 9:35). Listen to him. Listen. It is not enough to experience the glory of God in Jesus on the mountain. One must come down and go on. To listen to Jesus is to hear again a prediction of his death; to listen to Jesus is to embrace suffering and crucifixion. But to listen to Jesus is also to experience Easter.

With the hills of Samaria in the background, this path leads to the summit of the ancient city of Samaria.

26. Samaria

About the Site

The route to Jerusalem from Galilee offered several travel possibilities: one going along the east side of the Jordan, then up through Jericho; another going through Samaria, avoiding the valleys and hills of other routes. The journey through Samaria, though passing through unfriendly territory, took only three days.[1]

The name Samaria referred both to the ancient capital of the northern kingdom of Israel and, after its destruction in 722 B.C.E., to its outlying regions. The Assyrians, who destroyed Samaria and exiled thousands of its citizens, renamed their provinces according to the principal city. The Jezreel Valley on the north, the Aijalon Valley on the south, the coast to the west, and the Jordan River to the east formed the natural boundaries of Samaria,[2] an area about forty miles from north to south and fifty miles from east to west. Galilee lay directly north and Judea south.

Historical texts testify to the continual strife between Jews and Samaritans. Near the turn of the century, during the feast of Unleavened Bread, some Samaritans defiled the Temple by scattering human bones throughout. Between the years 48 and 52, Galilean pilgrims going to Jerusalem were slain by Samaritans, inciting brutal retaliation by the Jews. The Samaritans also suffered persecution under Pontius Pilate, who was banished in 36 because of his excessive cruelty.[3]

The town of Samaria, in the first century, had been rebuilt by Herod the Great and renamed Sebaste in Greek (Latin: Augusta) in honor of his patron, the emperor Augustus. No biblical texts indicate that Jesus

[1] John E. Stambaugh and David L. Balch, *The New Testament in Its Social Environment*, ed. Wayne A. Meeks (Philadelphia: Westminster, 1986) 94.

[2] James D. Purvis, "Samaria," *Anchor Bible Dictionary*, ed. David Freedman (New York: Doubleday, 1992) 5:914.

[3] John J. Rousseau and Rami Arav, *Jesus and His World* (Minneapolis: Fortress, 1995) 243.

went through the town of Samaria, though he did pass nearby at Sychar, which is the modern village of Askar. The distance from Sychar to Jacob's Well is less than a mile. Jacob's Well and the field once surrounding it had been given to Joseph by his father Jacob (Gen 48:22). Today the well still provides water to the thirsty pilgrim. At the edge of the busy city of Nablus, an indistinct metal gate in a long wall marks the entrance to an Orthodox church built over the well. The church was never completed, but a shelter was constructed over the well, and the caretaker happily escorts visitors down the steps to the well.

Reflection

Travel in the first century was not too different from what it is today. Along the road farmers would sell their produce to passersby. Inns provided beds and weigh stations provided fresh horses for imperial couriers. "Mansiones" had several bedrooms and stables for animals. Reserved for the traveling bureaucrats of the Roman Empire, these more elaborate facilities were located a day's journey apart, about twenty-five to thirty-five miles, depending on the terrain. Ordinary folk stayed at smaller stations about ten miles apart.[4]

The safest mode of travel was to rely on the Mediterranean cultural tradition of hospitality—providing food and lodging to visitors with the hope that that same hospitality would be extended to you in the future. When Jesus sent his disciples ahead of him, he was sending them with a request for hospitality. The Samaritans saw themselves as the true "Israelites," the remnant of the tribes of Ephraim and Manasseh who had survived the Assyrian invasion in 722 B.C.E.[5] Their holy mountain was Mount Gerizim, so Jewish pilgrims en route to Jerusalem would garner no sympathy from them. The Samaritans denied hospitality to Jesus and the disciples, not because they were Jewish, but because their destination was Jerusalem.

This story is often interpreted as a lack of hospitality on the part of the Samaritans; however, it may serve to underscore the religious differences between Jews and Samaritans and not their cultural ones. A Jew going to Jerusalem on pilgrimage was required to be clean, unsullied by contact with non-Jews, such as the Samaritans. Residing in their homes would have rendered Jesus unclean, and therefore unable to participate in the Temple functions.

Throughout the Gospels, the Samaritans appear on the fringe of the Good News. After John baptized Jesus, he moved north to Aenon near

---

[4] Stambaugh and Balch, *The New Testament*, 38.

[5] Robert T. Anderson, "Samaritans," *Anchor Bible Dictionary*, ed. David Freedman (New York: Doubleday, 1992) 5:940.

The lush garden outside the half-built church at Jacob's Well provides a quiet respite amid the noise and crowds of Nablus, or ancient Shechem.

Salim (John 3:23), which is in Samaria, indicating a baptizing ministry among the Samaritans.[6] When Jesus passed through Samaria, he encountered the woman at the well, engaging her in conversation (John 4). After healing the ten lepers, only the Samaritan returned to praise God (Luke 17:11-19). They were used as a startling example of mercy and kindness in the parable of the Good Samaritan (Luke 10:29-37). The Samaritans stood as the "other" in first-century Palestine, those who looked in but did not enter fully into the experience. They were insightful, thankful, compassionate, but never the ones for whom the message seemed to be directed. But even in the chance encounter with Jesus, they were changed.

The woman at the well engaged Jesus in a theological debate. "Sir, I can see that you are a prophet. Our ancestors worshiped on this mountain; but you people say that the place to worship is in Jerusalem" (John 4:19-20). And it is to this woman, this Samaritan, that Jesus announced, "I am he, the one who is speaking with you" (John 4:26), the long-awaited Messiah.

[6] Jerome Murphy-O'Connor, O.P., "Why Jesus Went Back to Galilee," *Bible Review* 12 (February 1996) 27.

Doubtlessly, Jesus saw his mission as pertaining to "the lost sheep of the house of Israel," but even he was changed by his encounters with the "other." While focusing on his original goal, he was still able to accommodate the unexpected conversion. The thankful leper. The enlightened woman. The neighbor who was a stranger no longer. In our world we too often seem surrounded by Samaritans whose inhospitality we take personally. What would our world look like if we saw in the face of the "other" the possibility of conversion and new life? What would our world look like if in that process the conversion happened to us?

Byzantine column bases jut out of the cool waters of the Pool of Siloam.

27. The Pool of Siloam

Scripture Reading

Cycle A   4th Sunday of Lent   John 9:1-41

About the Site

In Jerusalem, from the foot of the southeastern hill (Ophel) the Gihon Spring pours out into the west side of the Kidron Valley. The spring's name, Gihon, means "to gush forth" and was so called because of its intermittent action. Cool water bursts out from within a cave once or twice a day in the dry season, four or five times in the rainy season. This spring determined the location of a Canaanite village, the oldest known settlement in Jerusalem (1800 B.C.E.).

Sometime during this settlement a tunnel was dug from the spring westward into the hill and connected with a vertical shaft that came up inside the city walls, thus providing protected access to the water.[1] When David became king of Israel (1000–960 B.C.E.), he set out to capture Jerusalem from the Jebusites. These early inhabitants, claiming invulnerability, said to David, "You cannot enter here: the blind and the lame will drive you away!" (2 Sam 5:6). David's reply indicates how he took the city: "All who wish to attack the Jebusites must strike at them through the water shaft" (2 Sam 5:8). The area above the Gihon Spring came to be called the City of David.

In the time of Hezekiah, nearly three centuries later, water channels from the spring were used to irrigate the Kidron Valley for farmland. Under the threat of invasion by the Assyrians, all the channels were closed off except the one that brought water into the city (2 Kgs 20:20). This conduit, now called Hezekiah's Tunnel, was enlarged, providing an underground aqueduct winding through 1,749 feet of rock from the Gihon Spring to a reservoir inside the city called the Pool of Siloam. This name in Hebrew is Shiloah and is mentioned by Isaiah (Isa 8:6) in a reference to the impending capture by the Assyrians. In Arabic the name is Silwan. Today the Arab village that clings to the east side of the Kidron Valley is called Silwan. Though the Assyrians did eventually capture and destroy Jerusalem, the tunnel and pool remain to this day. The pool is the site of the miracle that healed the man born blind recounted in John 9:1-41.

[1] Jack Finegan, *Archaeology of the New Testament* (Princeton, N.J.: Princeton University Press, 1992) 188–192.

In the second century the Roman emperor Hadrian rebuilt Jerusalem and changed its name to Aelia Capitolina. In so doing, he attempted to wipe out all evidence of holy sites revered by Christians. Over the Pool of Siloam he built a shrine to nymphs. In the Byzantine period (fourth to seventh century), a domed basilica with two marble baths was located over the pool. Many cures were attributed to the waters within. This structure is included in the sixth-century Madaba map of Jerusalem, an indication that it was a significant church at that time.

As is true of most structures in the Holy Land, this basilica was destroyed by the Persians in the seventh century, and for more than a thousand years its location was unknown. Excavations toward the end of the nineteenth century recovered the site. A mosque was built over it, with a minaret rising above the present pool, which is fifty feet long and fifteen feet wide. Some still come from the village of Silwan to wash clothes in the pool.

Reflection

Many an adventuresome pilgrim has actually walked through the 1,749 feet of Hezekiah's Tunnel from its entrance at the Gihon Spring to its exit at the Pool of Siloam. There are a variety of reasons one might do this. Perhaps one might want to recall vividly the means by which David's army captured the city or experience firsthand this incredible 2,700-year-old engineering feat. One could imagine what it would have been like when the teams of workers that began digging at opposite ends met in the middle, or one might just want to explore one more contour of this amazing land. The water level in the tunnel varies at different times of the year, so one might emerge with dry clothes or soaked to the skin. Often the short-term memory of the walk through the tunnel is the somewhat silly feeling that goes with how wet one might have gotten. A more lasting memory, however, is that of the experience of a period of darkness and the struggle to wade through the resistance of the water in order to get to the light.

This image describes precisely the experience of the blind man whom Jesus cured on the Sabbath at the Pool of Siloam (John 9). This man's period of darkness lasted much longer than a walk through Hezekiah's Tunnel. He was an adult, blind since birth. After his cure he, his neighbors, family, and religious leaders struggled to understand what had happened and what could be the nature of the person responsible for the cure. Three times the man tells the details of how it happened: that he was blind but now he can see. With each telling of the story the man's faith in Jesus grows. After the first telling, his neighbors ask, "Where is he?" The man merely replies, "I don't know." After telling the story to the Pharisees, he is asked, "What do you have to say about him?" The man answered, "He is a prophet." By the end of the third repetition, the man, who hours before had been a blind beggar, engages in a theological debate with the Pharisees, asserting that Jesus must be from God if he is able to do these things. More than a bodily transformation has taken place in him; he has also gone through a struggle of coming to faith in Jesus.

The cure of the blind man is one of seven miracle stories in the first part of the Gospel of John (1:19–12:50). Each miracle is a sign that points to Jesus' identity with God. Before spitting on the ground to make the clay that he smeared on the man's eyes, Jesus identifies himself by saying, "I am the light of the world." The blind man moves from the miracle experience by which his sight was restored to true faith in Jesus, the light. The miracle has two sides: first, Jesus' healing power is used to bring people closer to God, and second, one must accept the invitation and believe that the source of the power is the goodness of a loving God. The blind man came to that faith; his parents and the Pharisees did not.

There are many forms of blindness and many simple people whose reflection of the goodness of God can lead us to the light. May we be open to those miracles.

The entrance to the Tomb of Lazarus is a steep and narrow descent into a first-century tomb.

28. Bethany

Scripture Readings

Cycle A	5th Sunday of Lent	John 11:1-45
	Trinity Sunday	John 3:16-18
Cycle B	4th Sunday of Lent	John 3:14-21
	Passion Sunday	Mark 14:1–15:47
Cycle C	16th Sunday of Ordinary Time	Luke 10:38-42
	Ascension	Luke 24:46-53

About the Site

The Mount of Olives is one of three peaks along a ridge that faces Jerusalem on the city's east side. A Russian church with a high tower provides a prominent modern landmark, making it easy to pick out the Mount of Olives even from a considerable distance. Southeast of the Mount of Olives along the same ridge is another, lower mount called Ras esh-Shiyah. Down the slope just a bit further is the present-day village of el-Azariyeh, or Bethany.

All four Gospels mention significant events in the life of Jesus that took place in Bethany. John 11:18 places Bethany two miles[1] from Jerusalem. Eusebius, a fourth-century bishop and historian, says that Bethany was at the second milestone from Aelia (Jerusalem) on a steep bank of the Mount of Olives.[2] The anonymous pilgrim from Bordeaux, writing in the fourth century, describes the village of Bethany as fifteen hundred paces eastward from the Mount of Olives. These references coincide with the present location of Bethany. It is here that the tomb of Lazarus can be found. Egeria, another well-known pilgrim of the fourth century, calls the village "Lazarium" and places it about fifteen hundred paces, or at the second mile, from the city. Egeria describes a liturgical celebration by the Jerusalem church at the Lazarium on the Saturday before Easter week:

> When they have come to the Lazarium the whole crowd assembles, so that not only the place itself, but the fields all around, are

---

[1] In some translations the distance is stated as fifteen stadia.

[2] Jack Finegan, *The Archaeology of the New Testament* (Princeton, N.J.: Princeton University Press, 1992) 155.

full of people. Hymns and antiphons are sung appropriate to the day and place, and in like manner readings suitable for the day are read. Before they are dismissed, Easter is announced. The priest goes up to an elevated place and reads the passage from the gospel where it is written, "When Jesus had come to Bethany, six days before the Passover" (John 12:1), etc. The passage having been read and Easter announced, they are dismissed. These things are done on this day because it is written in the gospel that so it was done in Bethany "six days before the Passover": now from the Sabbath to the fifth day, when, after the supper, the Lord was apprehended at night, is six days. Then they all return to the city straight to the Anastasis.[3]

The name Lazarium, given by Egeria, has developed into the Arabic name for this village, el-Azariyeh. Shaft tombs have been found in the area that date to the Canaanite period (1800 B.C.E.). Other finds, such as clay lamps, earthen pots of all kinds, many coins, including some from the first century, indicate that Bethany (el-Azariyeh) has been inhabited from 1500 B.C.E. through 1400.[4] Of the many tombs found in the area, one, with evidence of a church built over it, is revered as the tomb of Lazarus.

With the exception of modern plumbing, electricity, and automobiles, the village has not changed considerably since the fourth century. It is a relatively quiet residential village built on the slope of a steep hill. The bustling city of Jerusalem can be seen in the distance.

Reflection

Bethany, on the Mount of Olives, two miles from Jerusalem, was a significant place for Jesus. It is not known how often he came to Jerusalem or how he came to know Mary, Martha, and Lazarus. Being an observant Jew, he probably journeyed there to celebrate special feasts. During these times of pilgrimage the city's population would increase to several times its normal size, making housing difficult to find. It was certainly helpful to have friends with whom one could stay.

Bethany would have been a welcome place of refuge. Though not rural like Galilee, it was quiet and peaceful compared to the busy, crowded city of Jerusalem. Jesus found more than hospitality in Bethany—he also found friendship with Mary, Martha, and Lazarus. The intimacy and depth of this relationship are clear in the Lazarus

[3] P. Geyer, "Itinera Hierosolymitana saeculi," as quoted in Finegan, *The Archaeology of the New Testament*, 160.

[4] Finegan, *The Archaeology of the New Testament*, 157.

The Arab village of
El-Azariyeh preserves the
name of Lazarus.

story in the Gospel of John. When Lazarus became ill, the message sent
to Jesus by Mary and Martha was "Master, the one you love is ill"
(John 11:3). A couple of verses later, the Gospel writer reiterates, "Now
Jesus loved Martha and her sister and Lazarus" (John 11:5). When
Jesus arrived in Bethany to find Lazarus already buried, he wept (John
11:35). This is the only reference in the Gospels in which Jesus expressed grief due to a personal loss. These family members were his
good friends; Bethany was his home away from home.

The raising of Lazarus is one of many ironies found in John's
Gospel. The story is about giving life and is one of the seven signs that
Jesus gives us to explain who he is (John 1:19–12:50). This great sign of
life-giving was not just for Lazarus; we, too, need to be set free from
that which kills life in us. It is when we are with people who love us
that we can be our best selves and develop those gifts that others see
and call forth from us. Jesus' words "Untie him and let him go" (John
11:44) are spoken to us as well as to Lazarus. The irony mentioned earlier is that this life-giving miracle led directly to the decision of the
Sanhedrin to kill Jesus.

As Jesus' ministry progressed and he was noticed by the religious
leaders in Jerusalem, perhaps Bethany became a center for him where

people such as Nicodemus came to engage in discussion. In another ironic twist, Jesus' body was anointed by Mary at the house of Simon the leper (Mark 14). At a luxury dinner it would have been the custom that the hands and feet of the guests were washed and their body perfumed before the dinner began. Usually this would be done by servants, so it is significant that the anointing was done by Mary, who had sat as a disciple at Jesus' feet (Luke 10:38). Mark's Gospel is clear that the anointing of Jesus was a preparation for his death and burial. The anointing of the body before burial was a Jewish ritual. The exception was for criminals, who were not anointed before being buried. Jesus was about to suffer the kind of execution reserved for criminals. It must have been a powerful moment of understanding between Mary and Jesus when she poured the precious ointment on his feet.

Being among supportive and loving friends provides the opportunity to grow in self-knowledge and confidence. The time Jesus spent in Bethany with Mary, Martha, and Lazarus, people whom he loved and who loved him, perhaps contributed to the strength and courage he needed to understand, accept, and fulfill his mission. We all need to have friends, people with whom we can be at home. May we, too, be blessed as Jesus was with this precious ointment.

In the foreground, the wall of the Franciscan shrine follows the route of an ancient Roman road.

29. Bethphage

Scripture Reading

Cycle A	Passion Sunday	Matt 21:1-11

About the Site

About a mile east of the Temple Mount, the Arab village of Bethphage clings to the crest of a ridge on the Mount of Olives. It is midway between Bethany and the summit of the Mount of Olives. Archaeological studies done in the area of the Franciscan shrine indicate occupation from the second century B.C.E. until the eighth century. Saint Jerome attests to the presence of Bethphage in the fourth century when he mentions a visit made by Paula to the tomb of Lazarus at Bethany and then to Bethphage.

By the Crusader period, a chapel had been built over a block of marble from which pilgrims believed Jesus had mounted the colt. This stone was accidentally discovered in 1876. Five feet by four and a half feet by three feet, the stone has paintings on its various sides. The south side portrays the raising of Lazarus. The north side indicates a city wall, a group of men, and an ass and her colt. The east side shows people with palms. The west side bears an inscription referring to the ass and the village of Bethphage.[1] Interestingly, these sides roughly indicate the directions where these events occurred. Near the place where the stone was found, the apse of a Crusader church was also discovered. The Franciscans acquired the land and in 1883 built the current church enclosing the stone.

When pilgrims ascended from Jericho, they followed the Roman road through the long wadi Umm esh-Shid. When it reached the back of the Mount of Olives, this road separated into different routes over the ridge. The Franciscan shrine is located at the nexus of two of these ancient roadways. Though the exact location of ancient Bethphage is unknown, the church does mark the general vicinity.[2]

---

[1] Jack Finegan, *The Archaeology of the New Testament* (Princeton, N.J.: Princeton University Press, 1992) 165.

[2] Jerome Murphy-O'Connor, O.P., *The Holy Land* (New York: Oxford University Press, 1992) 136.

Reflection

Bethphage is mentioned several times in Talmudic literature, mostly in reference to the extent of the city limits of Jerusalem in which a sacred item might be prepared and used. In one reference the Mishnah states that an item must not be found "outside the wall." The exact meaning of "outside the wall" was a subject of debate among the rabbis. In the third century, Rabbi Johanan said this meant "outside the wall of Beth Page," indicating that Bethphage may have been a suburb of Jerusalem.[3] Hence entering Bethphage may, in fact, have meant entering the city limits of Jerusalem. Perhaps that is why Jesus chose to mount an animal at that point, for surely the most arduous part of the climb had been from Jericho. Though the Gospel writer paraphrases only part of Zechariah 9:9, his readers would have been familiar with the whole passage:

> Rejoice heartily, O daughter Zion,
>   shout for joy, O daughter Jerusalem!
> See, your king shall come to you;
>   a just savior is he,
> Meek, and riding on an ass,
>   on a colt, the foal of an ass.

While the Franciscan shrine at Bethphage today marks the beginning of the Palm Sunday procession, it may also mark the beginning of the procession of Jewish pilgrims who streamed into the Holy City for the feast of Tabernacles. This feast includes processions with palm branches as the people chant "Hosanna" ("O save now").[4]

> The other symbol of Succos as the Feast of Ingathering, is the cluster of plants—the lulav, esrog, myrtle and willow—with which the worshiper rejoices before God, as he chants praises of gratitude to the Giver of all good. Many are the symbolizations of the four species in this festive cluster. They have, for example, been taken to indicate different human types: the tall palm-branch denoting the men of power and influence; the aromatic esrog, the men of saintliness and learning; the myrtle, the average men and women of a community; and the willow representing the poor and lowly—but all of them forming one human Brotherhood mutually responsible for the welfare and good name of the whole.[5]

---

[3] Finegan, *The Archaeology of the New Testament*, 162.
[4] Joseph H. Hertz, *The Authorized Daily Prayer Book* (New York: Bloch, 1985) 792.
[5] Ibid.

The feast of Tabernacles or Booths is recorded in chapter 7 of the Gospel of John. One of the three pilgrim festivals in ancient Israel, it was also known as Sukkoth, after the Hebrew word for the tent erected: the *sukkah*. Occurring in the week following the first full moon after the autumnal equinox, the celebration was one of thanksgiving for the harvest as well as a remembrance of God's mercies shown to the Israelites in the wilderness.

A spirit of joy was the characteristic tone for the eight-day festival. "Joy is a fundamental note of the Jewish religious spirit, and happiness is a duty in Judaism," writes Dr. Joseph H. Hertz, a former chief rabbi of Britain.[6] During the Temple period, a procession to and from the spring that provided water for the sanctuary was accompanied by torch dances and songs and hymns by Levites and the people. According to Hertz, the Mishnah says, "He that hath not beheld the rejoicing at the Drawing of water, hath never seen rejoicing in his life."[7]

This story of Jesus' entry into Jerusalem may have originally occurred during the feast of Tabernacles and not during the feast of Passover, as the synoptic evangelists state. If so, it was in this festive spirit that Jesus entered the crowded city of Jerusalem. Probably he was surrounded by other pilgrims, and, indeed, they may have all been carrying palm branches. Today when Jews go to the Western Wall during Sukkoth, they carry their lulav and esrog in long, zippered plastic bags to prevent their being crushed by the masses.

The steep, ancient road runs beside the southern wall of the Franciscan shrine before blending into the modern asphalt that will incline sharply up the ridge to the Mount of Olives. Because the hike up from Jericho is tremendously steep and long, one does wonder why Jesus would have chosen to ride at that point. And indeed, it would seem that he had prearranged to have the animal waiting (Matt 21:2-3). From that point he would have ridden up a shorter incline, crested the Mount of Olives, and continued down into the Kidron Valley, where he would have entered the city by the Gate of Benjamin, according to Theodosius, a sixth-century pilgrim,[8] or entered directly into the Temple by the Shushan Gate.

Whether the palm branches were being waved in honor of Jesus or as part of a larger festival, certainly Jesus' joyous mood suddenly changed, for Matthew places the cleansing of the Temple immediately after Jesus' triumphant ride into the city. Jesus demonstrates that God's commandment of love means that one may be called upon to

---

[6] Ibid., 793.
[7] Ibid.
[8] Finegan, *The Archaeology of the New Testament,* 163.

speak the harsh word of truth, to wield a whip of justice, and to cleanse a way of worship caked with burdensome laws and choking obligations. But it begins first with a call from the people themselves: "Hosanna, save us."

Through a narrow alley, the Church of the Dormition is visible. In this area Jesus would have celebrated the Last Supper.

30. Jerusalem: The Upper Room

Scripture Readings

Cycle A		
	Holy Thursday	John 13:1-15
	2nd Sunday of Easter	John 20:19-31
	5th Sunday of Easter	John 14:1-12
	6th Sunday of Easter	John 14:15-21
	7th Sunday of Easter	John 17:1-11
	Pentecost	John 20:19-23
Cycle B		
	Holy Thursday	John 13:1-15
	2nd Sunday of Easter	John 20:19-31
	5th Sunday of Easter	John 15:1-8
	6th Sunday of Easter	John 15:9-17
	7th Sunday of Easter	John 17:11-19
	Ascension	Mark 16:15-20
	Pentecost	John 20:19-23
Cycle C		
	Passion Sunday	Luke 22:1–23:56
	Holy Thursday	John 13:1-15
	2nd Sunday of Easter	John 20:19-31
	5th Sunday of Easter	John 13:31-35
	6th Sunday of Easter	John 14:23-29
	7th Sunday of Easter	John 17:20-26
	Pentecost	John 20:19-31
	Trinity Sunday	John 16:12-15

About the Site

Outside the sixteenth-century walls of the Old City of Jerusalem, on the southwest side, is a hill known as Mount Zion. A two-story structure just a stone's throw from the city gates houses the Tomb of David on the lower level and the Cenacle, or Upper Room, on the second level. According to 1 Kings 2:10 and Nehemiah 3:16, David was buried in the City of David, that is, on the southeastern hill of Jerusalem. However, tradition that existed already in the first century[1] placed David's tomb on the southwestern hill, Mount Zion. The tradition was accepted by Muslims as well as Jews and Christians. The Jerusalem calendar of feasts (prior to 638) includes a celebration of David

---

[1] Jack Finegan, *The Archaeology of the New Testament* (Princeton, N.J.: Princeton University Press, 1992) 238.

on Zion on December 26. Today the Tomb of David is a Jewish sanctuary.

Excavations within and around this structure in 1951 uncovered an apse of dressed stones called "ashlars" dating to the first century. The apse is oriented to the Church of the Holy Sepulcher, leading to a supposition that this structure was a meeting place for Judeo-Christians. Descending levels of flooring can be dated to the Turkish, Crusader, and early Byzantine periods.

Mount Zion, the highest hill in Jerusalem, was the least destroyed by the Romans in 70. When Emperor Hadrian visited the city in 130, he found on Zion "the church of God, which was small, where the disciples, when they had returned after the Savior had ascended from the Mount of Olives, went to the upper room."[2] If the small church that Hadrian saw was at the place where the disciples stayed after the Ascension, one could suppose that the private home with the "upper room" where the Last Supper took place and the disciples gathered after the death of Jesus had been converted into a church. Both Nazareth and Capernaum had churches built over a place deemed to have been made holy by the presence of Jesus.

In Mark 14:15 and Luke 22:12, the Last Supper is said to have taken place in an "upper room." Acts 1:13 describes the disciples, after the Ascension, as staying in an "upper room." Jerome, in his Latin translation of the Bible, uses the word *cenaculum* (in English, "cenacle") in these passages. A cenacle was a dining room and was sometimes on the upper level of the house. It may be supposed, but not proven, that the two gatherings mentioned above were in the same place. Acts 2:1, the account of Pentecost, may possibly have taken place in the same "upper room." Mary, the mother of John Mark, was known to be a wealthy woman. Her home would have been spacious and could have been the gathering place of these earliest followers of Jesus. The centralizing of these events into a single place was affirmed in early tradition.

The current Cenacle is a fourteenth-century Franciscan restoration. The room is a hall forty-six feet long, thirty feet wide, and twenty feet high. There are two columns in the middle of the room, supporting a Gothic-type vaulted ceiling. A stairway in the southeast corner leads up to a small room, which is considered to be the place of the descent of the Holy Spirit.[3]

---

[2] Epiphanius (b. 315), as quoted in Finegan, *The Archaeology of the New Testament*, 233.

[3] Finegan, *The Archaeology of the New Testament*, 242.

Reflection

The disciples were gathered together with Jesus in a room somewhere in or near Jerusalem for the most significant events that preceded the passion and death of Jesus and also for those transforming events that occurred within a short time after the resurrection. Locating the exact place or determining which events actually happened here is not essential. However, focusing on the Upper Room as a specific place allows an overview of these events that would be missed if each of these Gospel readings were considered separately.

It was during this brief time, a few weeks only, that the basic concepts which define the Christian community were forged and initiated. Reconciliation, unity, service, and the Spirit who commissions us are the signs by which the Christian community will be known. Each of these signs was given to the disciples while they were together in the Upper Room.

In Middle Eastern culture, one does not share a meal with one's enemy. Eating together is a sign of intimacy, of welcoming, and, if appropriate, of forgiveness and reconciliation. It is significant, therefore, that the last time Jesus was with his disciples before his passion and death, his last instructions and prayers with them happened at a meal around a table. Jesus knew that he was dining with Judas, who would betray him, and Peter, who would deny him. In so doing, Jesus modeled for us a love that goes beyond worthiness, a love that is faithful in spite of failure and sin. There is, in this love, the willingness to be reconciled, which is one of the distinguishing characteristics of this new community.

All that happened during this meal was perhaps taken for granted by the participants as part of a ritual with which they were very familiar. It was only later that certain words and actions took on a greater importance. The special meal began with the blessing of the bread and the cup, a prayer that would have been prayed by everyone at the table.[4] Jesus referred to the bread as his body. At the end of the meal, Jesus blessed the cup again, this time saying that the cup was the new covenant in his blood (Luke 22:17-20). In this way Jesus used a common ritual to memorialize the gift of his life that would be broken and consumed, yet present among us whenever we break bread together in his name. The breaking and sharing of bread with wine became the sign of unity binding us to one another, to Jesus, and through Jesus to the Father.

---

[4] The Gospel of Luke identifies this last supper of Jesus with the apostles as a Passover meal (Luke 22:15).

The Gospel of John elaborates a different common ritual that also would have been performed at a formal meal. At the time of Jesus, one of the ways to welcome a guest was to provide for washing the dust of the road from the guest's feet. This act of kindness would have been performed by a servant, never by the host. Peter's reaction to Jesus' humble service to his guests is an indication of just how shocking it was for Jesus, the host, to perform this action. By washing the feet of his guests, Jesus turned upside down any notion of hierarchy in the social order. Jesus modeled for us a behavior of loving one another that eliminates status and allows us to give and receive from one another as a community of equals.

Reconciliation, unity, and service within a community of equals characterize the new community established by Jesus. But this community is not an isolated group of individuals who have followed and supported Jesus in his public ministry. This group of men and women do not comprehend what Jesus is telling them. They are devastated when he is arrested, tried, convicted, and executed in a matter of hours. Who could have imagined that this crew could be entrusted with the responsibility of sharing the mission and message of Jesus with the rest of the world?

Yet there was one more significant and transforming event that happened in the Upper Room. Perhaps it was on the Jewish feast of Pentecost, seven weeks after Passover, that the disciples were once again gathered together in Jerusalem. Within this time several had experienced an appearance of the risen Jesus. These appearances included a sense of mission, yet the disciples had the notion that the endtime was near, and they were looking for a further manifestation of this endtime. What they experienced was much more powerful. Just as the first human received life from the breath of God and the dry bones were revivified in the vision of Ezekiel (chap. 37), the closest disciples of Jesus collectively experienced an ecstatic spiritual presence of God's Spirit, a renewed sense of community, and a missionary impulse. The enthusiasm of the disciples and the power with which they delivered the message of Jesus from this day forward were strong forces attracting others to join them.

Reconciliation, unity, loving service among a community of equals, and the power of the Spirit who sends us forth to the whole world—these are the distinguishing signs of the community of followers of Jesus. The Upper Room is still our gathering place; it is wherever we are gathered in his name. There the power of the Spirit, the gift of the risen Jesus, is still alive in us.

A new walkway allows pilgrims to travel through the Kidron Valley and up to the Mount of Olives. The Church of All Nations at the Garden of Gethsemane is in the background.

31. Jerusalem: Across the Kidron Valley

Scripture Readings

| Cycle B | Good Friday | John 18:1–19:42 |
| Cycle C | Good Friday | John 18:1–19:42 |

About the Site

Jerusalem is built on a mount with three valleys surrounding it. On the west is the Valley of Hinnom, where garbage was burned, pagan gods were worshiped, and King Manasseh immolated his sons (2 Chr 33:6). It is called Gehenna in Matthew (5:22) and was the Jewish version of hell. The Tyropoeon Valley, also known as the Valley of the Cheesemakers, runs north to south and was the northern boundary of the ancient City of David. By the first century it had been enclosed within the city walls. Between the city on the east and the Mount of Olives is the Kidron Valley, a wadi or dry riverbed that floods during heavy rainfall. "Despite its narrowness, the Kidron is traditionally identified as the Valley of Jehosaphat, where Joel 3:2–4:12 places the gathering of all nations for judgment."[1] The three valleys come together in the south near Haceldama (Akeldama of Acts 1:19, the place where Judas fell to his death).

The name Kidron may mean "dark" or "not clear" because of sediment churned up when the wadi fills from the rains. Its northern end begins just west of Mount Scopus, near St. Stephen's Gate. At this point the valley is known in Arabic as Wadi Sitti Maryam, the Valley of St. Mary, since the traditional tomb of Mary is located there. Beyond the junction with the Valley of Hinnom, the brook of Kidron continues southeast into the wilderness of Judea before emptying into the Dead Sea. Silt and various accumulations have raised the valley ten to fifty feet since ancient times. Evidently the Kidron Valley was considered the eastern boundary of Jerusalem during the time of the United Kingdom.[2]

Because of Joel's prophecy, the valley has been, throughout the ages, a prime place for burial. Most striking of the thousands of tombs

---

[1] Raymond E. Brown, S.S., and Robert North, S.J., "Biblical Geography," *The New Jerome Biblical Commentary* (Englewood Cliffs, N.J.: 1990) 1190.

[2] W. Harold Mare, "Kidron, Brook of," *Anchor Bible Dictionary* (New York: Doubleday, 1992) 4:37.

in the valley are the Tomb of Absalom, the Tomb of Zechariah, and the Tomb of Pharaoh's Daughter, all of which are misnamed. The Tomb of Absalom, with its bottle-shaped top, was associated with David's son Absalom by Benjamin of Tudela (1170) on the basis of 2 Samuel 18:18: "Absalom in his lifetime set up for himself a pillar that is in the King's Valley," considered to be the Kidron Valley. Built in the late first century B.C.E., the structure has served as a tomb, but its original function was as a funerary monument, or nephesh, for the catacomb in the cliff behind it.[3] About 150 feet to the south, the Tomb of Zechariah dates to the second half of the second century B.C.E. An inscription identifies this funerary monument with the priestly family of Hezir, mentioned in 1 Chronicles 24:15. Further south the Tomb of Pharaoh's Daughter resembles a house with no windows. The rock was cut away from the hillside between the ninth and the seventh century B.C.E.[4]

Reflection

After the Last Supper, Jesus and his disciples, without Judas, begin the steep three-mile hike back to Bethany. The route from the upper city, where the meal probably occurred, would have taken them down the first-century steps outside the modern Church of Peter in Galli-cantu and into the Kidron Valley. The meal would have been over late at night, so as they begin the climb into the valley, they are surrounded by darkness. On either side of their path, the Kidron is literally filled with the shadows of tombs. At the valley's base the incline begins again. Before setting out over the Mount of Olives, other pilgrims would stop first at the garden known as Gethsemane to rest before the steep climb over the hill to Bethany. The word Gethsemane in Hebrew comes from "oil presses," indicating that the garden probably was an olive grove in the first century.

Jesus, having noticed Judas' departure and knowing the growing hostility among the religious authorities, sensed trouble. Unnerved by the walk through the cemetery, he stopped to pray. The Transfiguration may have prefigured this exodus moment for Jesus, but it was only in the dark of the garden that he came face to face with the reality of his possible death.

Between the cross and escape, Jesus needed only to climb the Mount of Olives. Gethsemane is just a couple of miles from the Judean Wilderness. He could have stopped at Martha and Mary's house in Bethany, gathered some provisions, and escaped into the monotonous

---

[3] Jerome Murphy-O'Connor, O.P., *The Holy Land* (New York: Oxford University Press, 1992) 123.
[4] Ibid.

hills of desert sloping into the Dead Sea. The Roman soldiers would not have pursued him.

The moment of surrender in Gethsemane was not the culmination of some random life, but rather the result of a steady, consistent march toward the city "that kills the prophets." If Jesus didn't fully understand the implications of his preaching and healing in the early days of his ministry, surely it became painfully clear with the death of his mentor and relative, John the Baptist. In fact, Scripture scholar Jerome Murphy-O'Connor, O.P., asserts that when the Gospels place Jesus in the Decapolis or the region of Tyre and Sidon, he was "escaping" the closing clutches of Herod, who had no jurisdiction over those areas.[5] It would seem, then, that Jesus did choose at times to avoid conflict and potential harm.

And interspersed with these "escapes" were times of solitude in which Jesus removed himself not only from danger but from the day-to-day ministry. Jesus chose at times to avoid conflict; he also chose to engage in deep prayer. As a response to this solitude, he came to understand that there would be a moment when avoidance would give way to the cross. One wonders what words of comfort Jesus prayed that night. Could the twenty-third psalm have been a source of strength? Certainly he had just walked through a valley of death.

> You guide me along the right path
> for the sake of your name.
> Even when I walk through a dark valley,
> I fear no harm for you are at my side;
> your rod and staff give me courage (Ps 23:3-4).

It would have been an easy way to the wilderness of escape. Certainly Jesus had his moments of hesitation. But he also pursued a vigorous prayer life. And it was in response to those moments of prayer, of being with his God, that he came to have the courage to stay.

---

[5] Jerome Murphy-O'Connor, O.P., "Jesus Goes to Jerusalem," lecture, École Biblique, Jerusalem, Israel, October 7, 1994.

Inside the Citadel Museum near the Jaffa Gate, various levels of strata are visible. Here Pilate would have resided when he was in Jerusalem.

32. Jerusalem: The Praetorium

Scripture Reading

Cycle B   34th Sunday of Ordinary Time   John 18:33-37

About the Site

During his arrest, Jesus was taken to Caiaphas, the high priest, and then sent to Pontius Pilate, the Roman prefect. The Praetorium was the residence of the prefect. In some passages the area is called Lithostrotos, a Greek word meaning "stone-paved area." In Hebrew it is called Gabbatha (John 19:13), meaning "elevated place." Another Greek word, *bema,* is used to indicate a judicial bench or platform. Though some question exists as to the actual location of the Praetorium, there is little doubt that this is where Pilate would have judged Jesus.

The most likely location was the palace of Herod the Great in the upper city, west of the Temple. Like all Herod's palaces, this one also served as a fortress in case his subjects would revolt against him. Three great towers marked the citadel of the palace. The towers were named Phasael, for Herod's brother killed in battle; Hippicus, for a friend also slain in battle; and Mariamne, for his favorite wife, whom he nonetheless killed. According to Josephus, the palace contained rooms for a hundred guests. The palace grounds, like all Herod's palaces, had elegant gardens and patios.[1]

After Herod's death and the deposing of his son, Herod Archelaus, the palace became the prefect's residence in Jerusalem. Normally the prefect resided in Caesarea Maritima, probably in a former Herodian palace as well. The prefect journeyed to Jerusalem for pilgrim festivals, when the possibility of Jewish revolt heightened. For this reason, some have suspected the Fortress Antonia next to the Temple as the rightful location of the Praetorium. The fortress, built on a higher ridge, afforded an excellent vantage point from which the Romans could watch the throng of pilgrims on the Temple platform. This fortress, rebuilt by Herod before 31 and named for his friend Marcus Antonius, had originally been a citadel. Herod the Great resided there while his new palace was being built.

Today only parts of Phasael's Tower remain and are visible within the Citadel Museum beside the Jaffa Gate. Archaeology done in the

[1] John J. Rousseau and Rami Arav, *Jesus and His World* (Minneapolis: Fortress, 1995) 151.

area under the Convent of the Sisters of Sion uncovered an extensive water system dating to the fortress. In 70 C.E. the Romans built a ramp over the rock-cut pool. The central bay of this ramp is called the Ecce Homo Arch, commemorating Pilate's statement "Behold the man" (John 19:5).[2] This arch crosses over the Via Dolorosa and is visible today. Archaeological efforts also found a large courtyard with stone slabs constructed over the pools in 135. These stone slabs, though considered by some to be the Lithostrotos, are not in their original location, and therefore this courtyard cannot be the area where Jesus was judged.[3]

Reflection

Christian pilgrims crowd the Old City of Jerusalem, particularly on Fridays. From the Holy Sepulcher they can rent a large cross and carry it through the packed streets, pausing at various markers to remember the Way of the Cross. This devotion, though attracting thousands annually, "is defined by faith, not by history."[4] Byzantine Christians followed a route that began on the Mount of Olives. During the Middle Ages the Franciscans initiated a route that began at the Holy Sepulcher. Many of the stations were given their present location as late as the nineteenth century. A more authentic route begins at the Citadel Museum, widely held as the location of the Praetorium, and travels east on David Street and north on one of the three market roadways, then west to Golgotha.[5]

Christians try to retrace the Way of the Cross of Jesus in an attempt to enter more fully into the experience of Jesus' passion. Whatever point at which they begin, the hope is that by walking in the vicinity they may catch a glimpse of those last, awful moments of Jesus' life. But to begin with the carrying of the cross is to start too late. The passion of Jesus began when the very people for whom he had come—the Jews—handed him over to Pilate, because they did not have the right to execute anyone (John 18:31).

The cruelty of Pilate is historically documented, but it was the cruelty of his own that scourged Jesus. The religious authorities feared that the Good News would upset their precarious relationship with the Empire. "If we leave him alone, all will believe in him, and the Romans will come and take away both our land and our nation" (John

---

[2] Jerome Murphy-O'Connor, O.P., *The Holy Land* (New York: Oxford University Press, 1992) 36.

[3] Rousseau and Arav, *Jesus and His World*, 13.

[4] Murphy-O'Connor, *The Holy Land*, 37.

[5] Ibid., 38.

11:48). They acted, understandably, in a manner of protection. "It is better for you that one man should die instead of the people, so that the whole nation may not perish" (John 11:50). Earlier another prophet had arisen, claiming to be the Messiah. The Roman response was violent and quick.

Because Jesus' message of liberation was one of justice, the political ramifications were too great. The religious authorities acted in what they deemed to be the best for their religion and their people. Caiaphas "prophesied that Jesus was going to die for the nation, and not only for the nation, but also to gather into one the dispersed children of God" (John 11:51-52). To say that the Jews killed Jesus is to miss the crisis of faith that faced many Jewish leaders. Theirs was a licit religion within the empire as long as it remained quiet and unobtrusive. This Jesus was anything but quiet.

How many times have we discovered ourselves in similar straits? We struggle with choosing the right way among many right ways. Is it not better for one to die for others? Isn't that what Jesus said (John 15:13)? Laying down his life for his friends, Jesus was laying down his life for the Jews as well as the Christians who would follow.

The front of the Church of the Holy Sepulcher evidences its tumultuous history.

33. Jerusalem: Golgotha

Scripture Readings

Cycles A, B, C	Good Friday	John 18:1–19:42
Cycle C	34th Sunday of Ordinary Time	Luke 23:35-43

About the Site

The name Golgotha is from the Aramaic *golgolta,* meaning "skull" (Matt 27:33; Mark 15:22; Luke 23:33; John 19:17). In Latin the word is *calvaria,* from which we get the name Calvary. It is the name of a place of execution near Jerusalem, so called either because skulls were left there or because the hill looked like a skull.[1] Arabs today use the word *ras* ("head") to mean any rocky projection, not necessarily head-shaped, so *golgolta* need only mean a rocky projection, not necessarily skull-shaped.[2] Eusebius puts Golgotha in Aelia (Hadrian's city built over a destroyed Jerusalem) north of Mount Zion.[3]

The crucifixion of Jesus took place in approximately the year 30. Between 40 and 44, Herod Agrippa increased the size of the city from 140 to 310 acres, thus enclosing Golgotha within the city walls. Christians and Jews fled Jerusalem at the time of the Jewish civil war and the destruction of the Temple (66–70), but it can be assumed that knowledge of Golgotha was fresh in their minds and would have been passed on to other generations.

A century after the death and resurrection of Jesus, the emperor Hadrian rebuilt the city of Jerusalem. His plan included a temple dedicated to Jupiter, Juno, and Minerva built, in an attempt to eradicate the holy sites of Christianity, over the site of the crucifixion. Two centuries later (325) another emperor, Constantine, in partnership with his mother, Helena, demolished the temple built by Hadrian and excavated the site in order to "display the most blessed place of the Savior's resurrection in a worthy and conspicuous manner."[4]

---

[1] Harold Mare, "Golgotha," *Dictionary of Biblical Archaeology,* ed. E. M. Blaiklock and R. K. Harrison (Grand Rapids, Mich.: Zondervan, 1983) 217–218.

[2] G. S. P. Freeman-Grenville, *The Basilica of the Holy Sepulchre in Jerusalem* (Jerusalem: Carta, 1993) 51.

[3] John Wilkinson, *Jerusalem as Jesus Knew It* (London: Thames and Hudson, 1978) 146.

[4] Eusebius, *Life of Constantine,* 3:25-40, as quoted in Wilkinson, *Jerusalem as Jesus Knew It,* 147.

Three crosses for rent rest on the roof of the Holy Sepulcher.

The Church of the Holy Sepulcher, first built by Constantine, has been destroyed and rebuilt many times. Excavations by Kathleen Kenyon (1962–1963) have revealed two facts: the area occupied by the church was outside the city wall of Jesus' time, and pottery finds show the area to have been a quarry. No excavation can prove that the site venerated today as Golgotha is authentic, but this archaeological evidence supports rather than disproves the tradition that the site is authentic. In 1976 further excavations in the church uncovered, for the first time in sixteen hundred years, what is most probably the site of crucifixions. A cone of gray rock about thirty-five feet high rises from the top of an incline where prisoners were brought for execution. This site was close to a busy thoroughfare leading from the city and within several feet of the wall that may have held spectators.[5]

As one enters the Church of the Holy Sepulcher today, a staircase immediately to the right of the entrance leads to the place called Calvary. The small area (approximately thirty-eight feet by thirty-one feet)

---

[5] Carl Armerding, "Church of the Holy Sepulchre," *Dictionary of Biblical Archaeology* (see note 1 above), 407–408.

Under the lit candles, the rock of Calvary is seen.

is divided into two naves—one Latin, the other Greek. Beneath the Greek altar the white limestone rock of Calvary is visible under plate glass. A silver disk, with an opening large enough to put one's hand through in order to touch the rock, commemorates the place where the cross of Jesus might have stood.

Reflection

For many pilgrims, a first visit to the Church of the Holy Sepulcher is not a religious experience. Thousands of people come every day to the place where our Lord and Savior, Jesus Christ, laid down his life for us, his friends. Some come weeping, some singing, many in a crowd of dazed travelers who are being whisked from place to place. One wonders if these visitors comprehend where they are. The church is not particularly clean, and the decor is unfamiliar to the Western eye, neither attractive nor welcoming. There is often a cacophony of sounds from dueling liturgical services going on simultaneously within the large, carved-up interior of the church. It is as if one has arrived at an energy center where the electrons and neutrons of different varieties of Christianity clash with one another. If one comes here with the expectation of a quiet moment of solitary prayer, it is not likely to be found.

Why do people come here? Christians come to touch Golgotha and the Tomb because the event that happened here, the death and resurrection of Jesus, defines our faith. Everything we believe flows from this center. To be a pilgrim is different from being a tourist. A tourist travels away from his or her center (home) to explore other lands, to learn, rest, or be entertained. A pilgrim, in contrast, journeys toward the center, the core of his or her faith. Usually the pilgrim journeys with others who are moving toward the same center. Prayer and many other events along the way, perhaps illness or danger, form the group into a community. The journey is important preparation for arrival at the center.

The pilgrims who come to Calvary today, together with all who have come before, are members of the same family in the faith. All have been drawn by their common belief in Jesus and their common desire to touch and be touched by the holiest, most significant place on earth for all Christians. To be here is to be immersed in the great mystery of divine love by which redemption has been won for us. God so loved the world that the Son was given for us.

Jerome Murphy-O'Connor expresses well the challenge of a visit to the Church of the Holy Sepulcher: "The empty who come to be filled will leave desolate. Those who permit the church to question them may begin to understand why hundreds of thousands thought it worthwhile to risk death or slavery in order to pray here."[6]

---

[6] Jerome Murphy-O'Connor, O.P., *The Holy Land* (New York: Oxford University Press, 1992) 49.

The Stone of Unction, dating to 1810, commemorates the anointing of Jesus' body for burial.

34. Jerusalem: The Tomb

Scripture Readings

Cycle A	Easter	Matt 28:1-10
Cycle B	Easter	Mark 16:1-8
Cycle C	Easter	Luke 24:1-12

About the Site

A spent quarry outside the city walls of Jerusalem was used as a burial place for Jews in the early part of the first century. Tombs were cut into the vertical west wall of the quarry and also around a bank of inferior cracked stone on the east wall. The tombs were of a type called *arcosolia*, with a vestibule leading to a chamber in which there was a funerary couch or ledge. Excavations in the 1960s found remains of ancient rock-cut tombs, thus verifying that this area was outside the city wall at one time.[1]

According to John 19:42, Jesus' body was buried in the place where he was crucified. Golgotha, then, was a name used for both the place of the crucifixion and the place of burial. The Church of the Holy Sepulcher is built over this quarry. The contribution of archaeology verifies that the site is compatible with the information given in the Gospels.[2] John 19:17 tells us that Jesus was crucified on a rocky, skull-shaped projection outside the city. Further, John 19:41-42 mentions that Jesus was buried in a tomb nearby. Some of the land close to the quarry was cultivated, growing vines, figs, carobs, and olives. Wind-blown seeds would have provided some green growth in the quarry area, which John refers to as a garden (19:41).

The strongest argument for authenticity of the site of Jesus' burial comes from tradition. Liturgical celebrations were held at the site until 66 C.E.,[3] when Jews and Christians were forced to leave the city. Though centuries had passed, the memory of the site had not dimmed when Constantine bore the double expense of removing the temple

---

[1] Jews could not be buried inside the city.

[2] These contributions include verification that the area was outside the city walls in the beginning of the first century and that the area has within it rock-cut tombs of the type used by Jews.

[3] Jerome Murphy-O'Connor, O.P., *The Holy Land* (New York: Oxford University Press, 1992) 49.

built by Hadrian (132–135) in order to build the first Church of the Holy Sepulcher.

The church that stands today was reconstructed by the Crusaders in the twelfth century. Its most recent renovation was the cleaning and restoration of the rotunda over the Tomb in 1996. The tomb monument today, called an "Edicule," dates from the nineteenth century. It was built by the Greeks after a fire destroyed the previous Edicule in 1808. The Edicule and the Holy Sepulcher inside bear little resemblance to the original tomb. Other examples of tombs from the first century still exist and indicate that the tomb used for Jesus would have been either a shelf with an arched ceiling *(arcosolium)* or a long, narrow rectangular recess in the wall *(kokhim)*. After a body had decomposed, the bones were placed in an ossuary, a stone box with a lid, which would be kept in the tomb. The shelf in the tomb could then be used again.[4] A tomb fitting either of these descriptions would be sealed by a stone rolled across its opening. Joseph of Arimathea, known to be prosperous, could have had this type of tomb prepared for himself.

Within the Edicule, the Holy Sepulcher itself is about six feet by six feet in size. On the right side is a marble slab five feet long by two feet wide and three feet high, intended to mark the burial place of Jesus. The space is very small, allowing at most three or four persons inside at one time.

Reflection

At the time of Egeria (381–384), the place where Jesus was buried was referred to as the Anastasis, a Greek word meaning "resurrection." The place of Calvary and the place of resurrection were within the same Constantinian structure, with an unroofed atrium between them. During the Easter services one moved physically from the place of death to the place of new life. A shift in spirituality over the centuries has caused the emphasis to change from death/resurrection to death/burial. How much more appropriate it would be for this church to be called the Church of the Resurrection rather than the Church of the Holy Sepulcher.

A first visit to the Church of the Holy Sepulcher is not exactly a religious experience. The curious or those without faith will not be moved or impressed by the surroundings. Indeed, some of the faithful are put off by the somewhat chaotic activities within the church. It is hard to be reverent when being jostled in a crowd. Every day thousands of people come to the place where Jesus rose from the dead. One beautiful and relatively peaceful section of the church is the Mary

---

[4] John Wilkinson, *Jerusalem as Jesus Knew It* (London: Thames and Hudson, 1978) 157.

Behind the tomb of Jesus are first-century, rock-cut tombs similar to the one in which Jesus would have been placed.

Magdalene Chapel, next to the Edicule (tomb). The location of this chapel is appropriate, given the significant role Mary Magdalene plays in every gospel account surrounding the resurrection. Except in the apocryphal Gospel of Peter (9:35–11:44), there is no description of the resurrection. What we do have in the synoptic accounts describing the events of Easter morning are the discovery of the empty tomb by the women bringing spices to anoint Jesus' body and the action taken by these women.

Mary Magdalene is named as the first one to discover the empty tomb and hear the words of explanation given by the angel. The reaction of Mary and the women who were with her is one of shock. The women were "utterly amazed," "trembling and bewilder[ed]," "terrified," "fearful yet overjoyed." Despite their fear, they took the message of the angel back to the other disciples: Jesus is risen. Perhaps the gospel writers have only women present at this most significant moment in history to emphasize the truth of the resurrection. The women could not have overcome the guards, they could not have rolled back the stone, and given their role in society at the time, they would not have had the political connections necessary to arrange to have the body of Jesus removed from the tomb.

So even though there were no witnesses to the resurrection of Jesus, the women's experience of the empty tomb must be our foundation for the reality of the resurrection. Without this foundation, our hearts and minds would not be open to all that followed: belief in the appearances of the risen Jesus to the disciples shortly after the resurrection, the descent of the Spirit at Pentecost, the commission to make disciples of all nations. It is Mary Magdalene, first among the apostles, who provides the bridge we must all cross to the heart of our faith. Jesus is risen. He is still with us.

The highway from Tel Aviv to Jerusalem makes a sharp left turn around the rocky ridge at Motza, just west of Jerusalem. No longer a village, Qoloniya-Emmaus is a suburb of Jerusalem.

35. Emmaus

Scripture Readings

Cycle A	3rd Sunday of Easter	Luke 24:13-35
Cycle B	3rd Sunday of Easter	Luke 24:35-48

About the Site

When the two companions in Luke 24 left Jerusalem after Jesus' crucifixion, they traveled about seven miles, or as some of the original texts read, sixty stadia (a stadium was 607 feet). Some manuscripts read 160 stadia, making the conversion more than eighteen miles. Because of the discrepancy and the lack of any archaeological evidence predating the Byzantine period, the location of Emmaus is unknown. However, four areas fit the description and/or commemorate the event: Qubeiba, about seven or eight miles from Jerusalem; Abu Ghosh, about eight miles; Qoloniya, about three and a half miles; and Latrun, eighteen miles. All four locations are northwest of the city of Jerusalem.

The Arab village of el-Qubeiba was designated as Emmaus as late as the fifteenth century, when the Franciscans located it there because of its distance from Jerusalem. Excavations done in the late 1800s revealed the remains of a Crusader basilica. Within these remains were older structures, perhaps Byzantine or maybe even Roman. The possibility of a first-century, Roman-style house encouraged some to think of this structure as "the house of Cleophas."[1]

Approximately the same distance from Jerusalem and west of el-Qubeiba is Abu Ghosh. Its original name was Qiryat Yearim, an Old Testament city where the ark of the covenant was housed between its rescue from the Philistines and its relocation to Jerusalem (1 Sam 7:2). In the second century, the Tenth Roman Legion camped here, probably guarding the main route between Jerusalem and the seacoast. A reservoir over the springs built by the Romans was later incorporated into a khan, or caravan stop, by the Muslims in the ninth century. The Crusaders, unaware of any Emmaus sites commemorated in the Byzantine period, marked off sixty stadia, located the nearest village, and built a church there.

[1] Jack Finegan, *The Archaeology of the New Testament* (Princeton, N.J.: Princeton University Press, 1992) 288.

Another site, Qoloniya, was known as Emmaus in the first century but is only a few miles from the city. According to Josephus, after the First Jewish Revolt (67–70) eight hundred soldiers were given land at Emmaus, thirty stadia from Jerusalem.[2] The presence of the soldiers engulfed the town, causing it to acquire a new name, Qoloniya, preserved by the Arabs until their relocation in 1948. The highway from Tel Aviv to Jerusalem makes a sharp left turn around the rocky ridge at Motza, just west of Jerusalem. No longer a village, Qoloniya-Emmaus is a suburb of Jerusalem.

Following the variant reading of 160 stadia, Byzantine Christians located Emmaus eighteen miles northwest of the city, an area today known as Latrun. Until the war of 1967, the Arab inhabitants of this area preserved the biblical name, Imwas, for Emmaus. This Emmaus has a long history, owing to its strategic location at the corner of three routes to Jerusalem from the coastal plain. A notable second-century Christian soldier and diplomat, Julius Africanus, requested that Emmaus receive the rights of a Roman city. With a new name, Nicopolis, the area was still designed as the Emmaus by Jerome, who in 386 said that it was "where the Lord made himself known to Cleophas in the breaking of bread, thus consecrating his house as a church."[3] Earlier, Eusebius had noted this area as the location of the gospel event. Until a plague in the seventh century, pilgrims venerated this village as the actual Emmaus. Crusaders erected a church on the site, but more for military reasons than religious ones. They were probably unaware that it had once served as the site of the Emmaus story. Today the remains of the Crusader fortress at the Cistercian monastery, a Crusader church a little north, and Roman baths are visible. The baths date to the period when Emmaus was made an imperial city. The church is built on top of the remains of a fifth-century Byzantine church. The area continues to be a strategic intersection where the Jerusalem highway crosses the north-south route between Ramallah and Ashqelon.

All these sites are located near or on the main highway connecting Tel Aviv and the green coastal plain with Jerusalem and its semi-arid hills. At the Latrun intersection, the highway begins to ascend the hills of Judea. As it nears the exit to Abu Ghosh, the incline steepens, and, finally, the elbow turn at Motza reveals the heights of Jerusalem, some twenty-five hundred feet above sea level. To walk from Jerusalem to any of these sights is to engage in a strenuous and steep hike, clinging to the edge of the highway along vertical cliffs and deep valleys.

---

[2] William Whiston, *The Works of Josephus* (Peabody, Mass.: Hendrickson, 1995) 761.

[3] Jerome Murphy-O'Connor, O.P., *The Holy Land* (New York: Oxford University Press, 1992) 329.

Reflection

Remembering the words of Jesus, the two disciples turned their back on the city that "kill[s] the prophets" (Matt 23:37) and began their journey home. Admittedly, they had hoped for a rescuer, someone "to redeem Israel" (Luke 24:21). Instead their hopes were hung on a cross. A devastating ending for a disastrous life. Only a few followers remained. Most, like these two, had returned to their homes and their former lives. Again, hopeless. The walk from Bethany (where Jesus and the disciples stayed when on pilgrimage to Jerusalem) to Emmaus consisted of a series of ups and downs, steep climbs and quick descents—so much like their recent experience. From Bethany, Jerusalem is the peak, with the hills of Judea then declining toward the coast. Such was their route, both physically and emotionally, a steady decline from the holy heights to the plain of the ordinary.

In their state of profound disappointment, the two were joined by a fellow traveler. They explained to the stranger their most recent experiences, and in so doing announced an early kerygma, though without confessional confidence. Interestingly, the stranger offended them by responding, "Oh, how foolish you are! How slow of heart to believe all that the prophets spoke!" (Luke 24:25). This remark, in the first-century world, would have been considered an insult. Yet the two companions listened to the stranger. In fact, they went a step further and extended hospitality to him.[4] "In the world of the Bible, hospitality was never about entertaining family and friends. Hospitality was always about dealing with strangers."[5]

The two men pressed the stranger to stay with them as the evening drew near. He declined, as part of the hospitality custom. Then they urged again. He relented and entered their home. Table fellowship was seen as "the litmus test of social solidarity. Eating together meant that a bond ran deep among all the participants."[6] In offering a meal, the two disciples participated fully in their hospitality ethic. What was out of the ordinary was the stranger who took the bread, blessed it, and distributed its pieces. In that moment of reversal—the stranger becoming host—they recognized him. Jesus became known in the breaking with social customs, in the upheaval of the expected.

---

[4] Douglas E. Oakman, "The Countryside in Luke-Acts," *The Social World of Luke-Acts,* ed. Jerome H. Neyrey (Peabody, Mass.: Hendrickson, 1991) 163.

[5] John J. Pilch and Bruce J. Malina, *Biblical Social Values and Their Meaning* (Peabody, Mass.: Hendrickson, 1993) 104.

[6] Bruce Malina and Richard Rohrbaugh, *Social-Science Commentary on the Synoptic Gospels* (Minneapolis: Fortress, 1992) 411.

What had been a rote repetition of their experience of his life, death, and resurrection now takes on the power of a true confessional kerygma. Empowered by their new belief, they rushed back to Jerusalem, despite the late hour and the arduous climb. There they met the others, all proclaiming experiences of resurrection, and in the proclamation, suddenly, he is in their midst.

How often in our own lives do we rub up against the stranger? That which burns in our hearts is often not joy but chagrin. The streets of the Old City of Jerusalem, like those of most cities, are crowded with strangers, with the blind, with beggars, with the crippled—unlikely messiahs in a tumultuous time. Yet in their comely appearance, they, too, have the possibility of witnessing to the resurrection, if we but first welcome them in.

(Matt 16:13; Mark 8:27-29), he was in the tetrarchy of Herod Philip in Upper Galilee.

When the Gospel of Matthew speaks of a mountain in Galilee where the disciples experienced Jesus after the resurrection (28:16), a specific location is not given. Though the hills of Lower Galilee do not qualify as "mountains," this was the arena of Jesus' ministry. While Upper Galilee is truly mountainous, Jesus seems to have visited this area only on occasion. It is likely, then, that the mountain which Matthew refers to is one of the numerous hills bordering the western side of the Sea of Galilee, the locus of much of Jesus' work.

Mount Arbel and the Mount of the Beatitudes (see p. 88) are two summits near Capernaum. Mount Arbel towers above the Wadi el-Haman, or Valley of the Pigeons, where the ancient road from Nazareth passed on its way to Magdala. Here in its caves Herod the Great killed highwaymen who may have been attacking the caravans en route. The steepness of Mount Arbel, its violent history, and its rugged terrain make it an unlikely candidate for the mount of the resurrection encounter. The mount from which Jesus uttered the Beatitudes is referred to by Matthew as simply "the mountain" (5:1), the same designation used in 28:16. This gently sloping hill, with a commanding view of the lake and the whole of Galilee, makes a much better location for commissioning.

Reflection

The Sea of Galilee, so central in the life of Jesus, looks today very much as it did nearly two thousand years ago. Fishermen in small boats ply its waters, ever watchful for the sudden afternoon storms. Only Tiberias is large enough to be called a city. Gospel villages like Capernaum, Magdala, and Bethsaida are only archaeological sites now. The Mount of Beatitudes is a green, sloping hill, rolling into the banks of the sea. For visitors to the Holy Land, Galilee holds peace and promise, for here you can more easily imagine the world of Jesus.

Though heavily populated with Jews in the time of Jesus, Lower Galilee carried a reputation as a place "of the Gentiles" (Isa 8:23; Matt 4:15). The Jews of Judea looked with disdain on the Jews from Galilee, considering them less religious. Galileans were also less sophisticated. They were farmers from the hill country or fishermen from the lake. Even their accent gave them away (Matt 26:73). Among Galileans there were rivals and differences: "Can anything good come from Nazareth?" (John 1:46).

But it was to this place, not the holy city of Jerusalem, that the risen Lord sent his disciples: "Do not be afraid. Go tell my brothers to go to

36. A Mountain in Galilee

Scripture Readings

Cycle A	Ascension	Matt 28:16-20
Cycle B	Trinity Sunday	Matt 28:16-20

About the Site

Galilee, which in Hebrew means "circle," was both a geographic and political region in the first century. Today it extends thirty to forty miles from north to south and twenty to twenty-five miles east to west. The geographic area divides into Lower and Upper Galilee along an east-west fault line roughly between Acco on the coast and the northern edge of the lake to the east. Lower Galilee has a series of gentle hills rising no more than two thousand feet. The valleys have rich soil and continue to be highly cultivated, as they were in the first century. The villages climb the hills, leaving the more level ground for farming.[1] Directly north of the region of Samaria was the tetrarchy of Herod Antipas in the first century.

The largest body of water in Lower Galilee is called by several different names in the Scriptures. Chinnereth in the Old Testament (Gennesaret in Luke's Gospel) means "lyre-shaped," and the contours of the lake look like an upside-down harp laid north to south. Called the Sea of Galilee by Matthew, Mark, and John, the lake, at its widest point, is seven miles; it is twelve and a half miles from north to south. Its source is the Jordan River, which pours into its northern end. The same river drains it on its way to the Dead Sea farther south. Surrounded by hills on its west and the Golan Heights on its east, the lake suffers from sudden and unexpected storms. Little forestation and less habitation allow an overall view. From most points the entire circumference is visible.

Upper Galilee is the beginning of the Lebanon Mountain chain, with heights climbing from three thousand to four thousand feet. Heavy rainfalls, gusty winds, and steep mountains often made Upper Galilee a place of refuge.[2] When Jesus traveled to Caesarea Philippi

---

[1] Raymond E. Brown, S.S., and Robert North, S.J., "Biblical Geography," *The New Jerome Biblical Commentary* (Englewood Cliffs, N.J.: Prentice Hall, 1990) 1195.

[2] Ibid.

Galilee, and there they will see me" (Matt 28:10). In Matthew, the point of the resurrection encounter, the point at which the doubtful disciples are commissioned to be the bearers of the Word to the world, is right in their own backyard. And from there they are called to "make disciples of all nations" (28:19).

The Good News of Jesus, through the experience of resurrection, transcends the boundaries of neighborhood and religion and even ethnic identity.[3] Far from being a private revelation for a specific group, the Good News is meant to be shared. But Jesus knows how hard discipleship is and promises: "Behold, I am with you always, until the end of the age" (Matt 28:20). The promise continues.

---

[3] The word translated as "gentile" in the New Testament comes from the Greek word *ethnos*, meaning "nation." It is from this word that we derive the English word "ethnic."

Bibliography

Achtemeier, Paul J., ed. *Harper's Bible Dictionary.* San Francisco: Harper & Row, 1985.

Aharoni, Yohanan, and Michael Ave-Yonah. *The Macmillan Bible Atlas.* New York: Macmillan, 1968.

Baly, Dennis. *Basic Biblical Geography.* Philadelphia: Fortress, 1987.

Barrett, C. K. *The Gospel According to St. John: An Introduction with Commentary and Notes on the Greek Text.* London: SPCK, 1978.

Beane, Wendell, and William Doty, eds. *Myths, Rites, Symbols: A Mircea Eliade Reader.* New York: Harper & Row, 1975.

Beitzel, Barry J. "The Via Maris in Literary and Cartographic Sources." *Biblical Archaeologist* 54 (June 1991) 64–75.

Brown, Peter. *The Cult of the Saints: Its Rise and Function in Latin Christianity.* Chicago: University of Chicago Press, 1981.

Brown, Raymond E., S.S. *The Birth of the Messiah.* New York: Doubleday, 1993.

Brown, Raymond, S.S., Joseph Fitzmyer, S.J., Roland Murphy, O.Carm., eds. *The New Jerome Biblical Commentary.* Englewood Cliffs, N.J.: Prentice Hall, 1990.

Brownrigg, Ronald. *Come, See the Place: The Ideal Companion for All Travellers to the Holy Land.* London: Hodder and Stoughton, 1985.

Brueggemann, Walter. *The Land.* Philadelphia: Fortress, 1977.

Charlesworth, James. *The Old Testament Pseudepigrapha.* New York: Doubleday, 1983.

Dillard, Annie. *Teaching a Stone to Talk.* New York: Harper & Row, 1982.

Eliade, Mircea, ed. *The Encyclopedia of Religion.* New York: Macmillan, 1987.

_____. *The Sacred and the Profane.* New York: Harper & Row, 1959.

Finegan, Jack. *The Archaeology of the New Testament: The Life of Jesus and the Beginning of the Early Church.* Princeton, N.J.: Princeton University Press, 1992.

Freedman, David Noel, ed. *The Anchor Bible Dictionary.* Vols. 1–6. New York: Doubleday, 1992.

Freeman-Grenville, G.S.P. *The Holy Land: A Pilgrim's Guide to Israel, Jordan and the Sinai.* New York: Continuum, 1996.

Harpur, James. *The Atlas of Sacred Places.* New York: Henry Holt, 1994.

Hennessy, Anne, C.S.J. *The Galilee of Jesus*. Rome: Editrice Pontificia Universita Gregoriana, 1994.

Hoppe, Leslie J. *Joshua, Judges*. Wilmington, Del.: Michael Glazier, 1982.

Jabusch, Willard. *Walk Where Jesus Walked*. Notre Dame, Ind.: Ave Maria, 1986.

Johnson, Luke Timothy. *The Gospel of Luke*. Sacra Pagina Series. Collegeville, Minn.: The Liturgical Press, 1991.

Johnson, Sherman E. *Jesus and His Towns*. Good News Studies. Wilmington, Del.: Michael Glazier, 1989.

Lane, Belden C. *Landscapes of the Sacred*. New York: Paulist Press, 1988.

Laymon, Charles M., ed. *The Interpreter's One-Volume Commentary on the Bible*. Nashville: Abingdon, 1971.

Malina, Bruce. *The New Testament World: Insights from Cultural Anthropology*. Louisville, Ky.: Westminster/John Knox, 1993.

Malina, Bruce, and Richard Rohrbaugh. *Social-Science Commentary on the Synoptic Gospels*. Minneapolis: Fortress, 1992.

Matthews, Victor. *Manners and Customs in the Bible*. Peabody, Mass.: Hendrickson, 1988.

Mays, James Luther, ed. *Harper's Bible Commentary*. New York: Harper & Row, 1988.

McRay, John. *Archaeology and the New Testament*. Grand Rapids, Mich.: Baker, 1991.

Meier, John P. *Matthew*. New Testament Message. Wilmington, Del.: Michael Glazier, 1980.

Meinardus, Otto. *The Holy Family in Egypt*. Cairo: American University Press, 1963.

Miller, Max. *Introducing the Holy Land*. Macon, Ga.: Mercer University Press, 1982.

Murphy-O'Connor, Jerome, O.P. *The Holy Land*. New York: Oxford University Press, 1992.

————. "Why Jesus Went Back to Galilee." *Bible Review* 12 (February 1996) 21.

Newsom, Carol, and Sharon Ringe, eds. *The Women's Bible Commentary*. Louisville, Ky.: Westminster/John Knox, 1992.

Neyrey, Jerome H., ed. *The Social World of Luke-Acts*. Peabody, Mass.: Hendrickson, 1991.

Ousterhout, Robert, ed. *The Blessings of Pilgrimage*. Chicago: University of Illinois Press, 1990.

Petrozzi, Maria Teresa. *Ain Karem: The Holy Places of Palestine*. Jerusalem: Franciscan Printing Press, 1971.

Pilch, John J., and Bruce J. Malina. *Biblical Social Values and their Meaning: A Handbook*. Peabody, Mass.: Hendrickson, 1993.

Pixner, Bargil, O.S.B. *With Jesus Through Galilee*. Rosh Pina, Israel: Corazin, 1992.

Rousseau, John J., and Rami Arav. *Jesus and His World*. Minneapolis: Fortress, 1995.

Satran, David. *Biblical Prophets in Byzantine Palestine: Reassessing the Lives of the Prophets*. New York: Brill, 1995.

Schüssler-Fiorenza, Elisabeth. *Searching the Scriptures: A Feminist Commentary*. New York: Crossroad, 1994.

Smith, Jonathan Z. *To Take Place: Toward Theory in Ritual*. Chicago: University of Chicago Press, 1987.

Stambaugh, John, and David Balch. *The New Testament in Its Social Environment*. Philadelphia: Westminster, 1986.

Stuhlmueller, Carroll, C.P. *Biblical Meditations for Ordinary Time*. Ramsey, N.J.: Paulist, 1984.

_____, ed. *Collegeville Pastoral Dictionary of Biblical Theology*. Collegeville, Minn.: The Liturgical Press, 1995.

Thomson, William. *The Land and the Book*. New York: Harper, 1886.

Vilnay, Zev. *The Guide to Israel*. Jerusalem: Sivan, 1964.

Weiser, Francis X., S.J. *The Holy Land: A Pilgrim's Description in Word and Picture*. Collegeville, Minn.: The Liturgical Press, 1965.

Whiston, William. *The Works of Josephus*. Peabody, Mass.: Hendrickson, 1995.

Wijngaards, John. *My Galilee, My People*. Mahwah, N.J.: Paulist Press, 1995.

Wilken, Robert. *The Land Called Holy: Palestine in Christian History and Thought*. New Haven, Conn.: Yale University Press, 1992.

Wilkinson, John. *Egeria's Travels Newly Translated with Supporting Documents and Notes*. London: SPCK, 1971.

_____. *Egeria's Travels to the Holy Land*. Jerusalem: Ariel, 1981.

_____. *Jerusalem as Jesus Knew It*. London: Thames and Hudson, 1978.